HISTORIC SHIPS
OF
SAN FRANCISCO

*A Collective History
and Guide to the Restored
Historic Vessels of the
National Maritime Museum*

STEVEN E. LEVINGSTON

Chronicle Books • San Francisco

Library of Congress Cataloging in Publication Data

Levingston, Steven E.
  Historic ships of San Francisco.

  Bibliography: p. 123
  Includes index.
    1. National Maritime Museum (U.S.). 2. Navigation—California—San Francisco Region—History. 3. Ships—California—San Francisco Region—History. 4. San Francisco Region (Calif.)—History, Naval.
  I. Title.
  V13.U6S265 1984   623.8'22'074019461   84-9410
  ISBN 0-87701-284-9

Editing: Carey Charlesworth
Book and cover design: Sharon Smith
Composition: Accent and Alphabet

10 9 8 7 6 5 4 3 2 1

Chronicle Books
870 Market Street
San Francisco, CA 94102

Photo Credits

Keith Adams page 92
A.O. Carpenter page 58
Russell Fraser page 103
Richard Frear page 99
Karl Kortum pages 12, 14, 15, 16, 18, 21, 24, 32, 33, 35, 36, 68, 71
Gabreille Moulin page 42
National Maritime Museum pages 23, 26, 28, 30, 40, 41, 42, 45, 47, 49, 52, 54, 56, 57, 58, 60, 61, 63, 64, 65, 66, 73, 75, 77, 78, 81, 82, 83, 84, 86, 88, 90, 99, 106, 108, 111, 116, 118
New England Ship Corporation page 94
William Letts Oliver page 57
Palmer Pictures page 40
Captain Persson pages 26, 38
Harry Piedgeon page 47
Frank Ricci page 28
Joanie Redington page 100
Richard Turner page 106

Table of Contents

For Mom, Dad and Sharon

Acknowledgments

I would like to express thanks and appreciation to Karl Kortum and the staff of the National Maritime Museum, San Francisco, for their boundless generosity and encouragement and permission to quote liberally from the museum's archival materials; David Nelson and the National Maritime Museum Association; the folks at the Golden Gate National Recreation Area headquarters and at the Hyde Street Pier; the people at the National Liberty Ship Memorial; Roger Olmsted, for writing such an exhaustive master's thesis on scow schooners of San Francisco Bay; Joan and Clay Blair, Jr., for preserving *Pampanito*'s rescue of POWs in their thorough and compassionate account *Return from the River Kwai;* Marjorie Levingston, whose computer wizardry saved me hours of work; and George Arndt and the staff of TSP Associates, for their patience and sophistication in the preparation of the manuscript.

Foreword

FOR CENTURIES THE UNITED STATES depended upon ships alone as the connecting links of empire. Yet even in those days of total dependence ships were more than items of pragmatic concern; the sea and the ships that have crossed it have been the subject of passionate interest. Fact and fiction in print have developed a rich international maritime literary heritage with Conrad, Dana, Marryat, Melville and Monsarrat, masters of the genre, joined by such authors more popularly known for other subjects as Poe, Defoe and Longfellow in creation of evocative tales of seafaring. Today, in more modern times, *ciné monde* maintains mankind's bond to the sea with such films as *Mutiny on the Bounty, Moby Dick, Captains Courageous, Titanic, Das Boot* and *Lifeboat*.

The real significance of ships transcends all of this. We can admire ships in print and on celluloid, but we can never truly experience a ship until we tread her decks, feel the ocean swell as the vessel rocks in the cradle of the deep and smell the salt air. No model, no painting, no photograph and no description, no matter how vivid, can replace the real thing. Realizing this, a handful of perceptive maritime historians and museum curators have challenged the traditional role of maritime museums; rather than calling for showcases of inanimate paintings and models, these bold pioneers have called for living enclaves where floating ships form the nuclei of collections that interpret America's seafaring heritage with actual artifacts from the days of sail and early steam. Now, many museums across the country have one or more ships preserved in their collections. In cases where these ships could not be saved afloat they have been placed on dry land to meet the future; others, a long list of rugged examples of their kinds still afloat, survive to remind the present and future generations of their nautical past. These ships include the famous U.S.S. *Constitution,* "Old Ironsides"; the 1885 square-rigger *Wavertree,* gem of the New York South Street Seaport's fleet; *Star of India,* an 1869 Cape Horner enshrined in San Diego; and the 1840 whaler *Charles W. Morgan,* which floats along with dozens of other vessels in Connecticut's exemplary Mystic Seaport. These hardy old salts have proved so popular that vessels sunk to their graves long ago have been resurrected from the deep for restoration and display around the world. The best known is the Swedish warship *Wasa,* which sank in Stockholm harbor in 1628 and was raised intact in 1961. In 1982 Henry VIII's warship *Mary Rose,* progenitor of the modern British Navy, was raised after 437 years on the bottom of The Solent. From the Mediterranean, archaeologists recovered and restored ship fragments to recreate a trading vessel that foundered 23 centuries ago off Kyrenia, Crete. And, in the United States, the Great Lakes schooner *Alvin Clark,* which capsized in a squall on Green Bay, Lake Michigan, in 1864, was raised intact in 1969. Now maritime archaeologists and historians are hungrily eyeing the perfectly preserved hulks of *Hamilton* and *Scourge,* American warships that sank in a Lake Ontario squall in 1813 while enroute to fight the British.

Prominent among the ranks of ship museums is the fleet of historic vessels moored on the San Francisco waterfront at the foot of Hyde Street. One of the largest floating collections of ships in the world, San Francisco's historic ships recall the rich and varied maritime history of the West Coast and of the city by the Golden Gate, once one of the principal harbors and ports of call of the world. Discovered accidentally by an overland hunting party of Spanish explorers in 1769, San Francisco Bay, previously navigated solely by the tule *balsas* of the region's aboriginal inhabitants, was entered by a European vessel for the first time in 1775. On August 5, the *paquetbot San Carlos* cautiously sailed through the narrow Golden Gate and anchored between Angel Island and the Tiburon peninsula. Where the *San Carlos* pioneered other Spanish ships followed, as San Francisco became the northernmost outpost of Spain's imperial expansion. The Presidio de San Francisco and the nearby Misión de San Francisco de Asís (later known as the Misión de los Dolores) were also occasionally visited by the far-ranging vessels of other imperial powers. In 1792, English explorer George Vancouver visited San Francisco in H.M.S. *Discovery*; in 1806 Russian nobleman Nikolai Petrovich Rezanof came in the *Juno* to request Spanish aid for Russia's starving Alaskan colonies. In 1814, H.M.S. *Raccoon,* cruising the Pacific while at war with the United States, was careened in Ayala Cove on Angel Island to repair damage incurred in crossing the Columbia River Bar. The *Raccoon*'s name remains today, designating the straits that separate Angel Island from the Marin mainland.

Trade between California and visiting foreign vessels began as the rich and fertile coastal plains were divided into large ranchos for the raising of tremendous herds of cattle. Known as the hide and tallow trade, since the only valuable trade commodities California possessed were the hides of slaughtered cattle and their fat rendered into tallow for soap and candles, this commerce brought dozens of vessels to the region's shores and, on them, increasing numbers of Americans who gradually settled along the coast. As the overseas need for California's "rawhide dollars" increased, San Francisco Bay became one of the principal ports of call, with a small hide trade outpost being established in 1835 along the muddy shores of the San Francisco peninsula. Known as Yerba Buena, the tiny settlement would eventually grow into the city of San Francisco.

Early on, California was an outpost of Mexico, that nation having won its independence from Spain in 1821 and acquired California as a province. But then the United States and Mexico went to war. On June 9, 1846 sailors and marines from the U.S.S. *Portsmouth* landed on the shores of Yerba Buena and claimed San Francisco Bay for the United States. From that point on the fortunes of California and its conqueror were one. Shortly the fates of both were altered, for on January 24, 1848 James Marshall, foreman of a group of laborers constructing a sawmill on the American River in California's Sierra foothills, spotted a sun-struck fleck of gold in the millrace. Marshall's fortuitous discovery sparked an unparalleled seaborne and overland migration to the western shore of the continent: the gold rush.

In 1849 alone 777 ships of every conceivable size, rig, and registry set sail from the ports of the world for San Francisco, the gateway to the gold fields. This incredible fleet and a great tide of humanity were thus deposited on the shores of the town formerly called Yerba Buena, which had taken the name of the bay two years previously to capitalize on the worldwide recognition of that inland sea as a great harbor. The results were phenomenal; San Francisco became an instant city as the crowded village metamorphosed into one of the nation's largest urban centers. So rapid was the growth that the city overran its shallow waterfront as well as many of the ships anchored there, which had been abandoned by gold-mad crews. These ships were converted into floating buildings, adding a distinctly maritime flavor to San Francisco's gold-rush-era architecture.

San Francisco was a city closely tied to the sea and to ships; this fact was perceived in 1852 by visiting Chilean journalist Benjamin Vicuña-Mackenna. To Vicuña-Mackenna, the city was

> as unique in the world as Venice is in Europe; it is a Venice built of pine instead of marble. It is a city of ships, piers, and tides. Large ships with railings a good distance from the beach served as residences, stores, and restaurants. I saw places where the tide had flowed down the street, turning the interior of houses into lakes. The whole central part of the city swayed noticeably because it was built on piles the size of ships' masts driven down into the mud. . . . Ships, the largest I have ever seen, were unloading merchandise from all over the world; Chinese silks, timber from Norway, flour from Talcahuano, and articles from Paris.

The boom market of the gold rush introduced millions of dollars of merchandise for trade to California and San Francisco, almost all of it carried in the holds of the large ships and steamers that daily discharged their loads on the city's shaky piers and wharves. California was isolated from the world and perched on the edge of the continent. With no industry or agriculture to speak of and the majority of the population in the mines, its lifeline was the sea.

The economic conditions of the gold rush brought maritime trade and commerce to San Francisco on a great and unparalleled scale. Eventually, though, as the human tide of argonauts ebbed, new factors arose that changed the character of shipping. By the 1860s California was no longer solely a consumer; the state had begun to produce valuable commodities in exchange for the goods imported to the region's greatest port, San Francisco. In the wake of the bluff-bowed whalers, sleek clippers and sidewheel steamers that had come in years past, there sailed iron-hulled British square-riggers carrying coal and other goods to trade for California grain grown in the San Joaquin Valley. In 1881, 559 ships, part of the grain fleet, loaded California's new golden product on the San Francisco waterfront. General cargoes were carried to and from the city in the holds of large, full-bodied wooden ships and barks built in New England after the Civil War.

These ships, many of which hailed from Maine, were known as downeasters. Ultimately, many of the downeasters made San Francisco their home port. They were joined by the New England whaling fleet, which relocated to the Pacific as Atlantic hunting grounds were exhausted and older whaling ports such as New Bedford and Nantucket declined. New whaling grounds in the North Pacific and the Arctic revived the industry and made San Francisco the undisputed major whaling port in the world. Closer to home, along California's rocky shores, a booming coastal trade brought local goods, usually produce and timber, to San Francisco. Small, easily maneuvered schooners often loaded lumber with wire chutes while anchored close to shore in narrow little inlets called dogholes, and other schooners plied the bays, esteros, and inlets of California's Point Reyes and Half Moon Bay ranches to bring butter, hay, firewood, eggs, and produce to market.

In addition to the lumber, whale oil, coal, produce and other merchandise landed on San Francisco's shores, another commodity—human freight—also passed through the Golden Gate, in the staterooms, cabins and holds of arriving vessels. The earliest had come via Cape Horn; during the first days of the gold rush thousands of people had navigated the treacherous tip of South America. By 1850 steamers operated by the Pacific Mail Steamship Company and their occasional competitors carried more than 500,000 souls who had crossed the steamy Isthmian jungles of Central America at Panama and Nicaragua to San Francisco. In the rough and rugged frontier atmosphere of the gold rush, these early steamers usually provided a luxurious and reliable means of transportation to California, and such steamers as the *John L. Stephens, Golden Gate, Tennessee* and *Brother Jonathan* quickly became lasting favorites. Even after the completion of the transcontinental railroad in 1869, ships continued to carry large numbers of passengers from Europe and the eastern seaboard to San Francisco. In the 1880s and 1890s increasing numbers of immigrants arrived from the Orient, oftentimes facing racist hysteria and xenophobia as hundreds rallied to the cry that "The Chinese must go!" Sadly, another aspect of San Francisco's maritime heritage was tied to that paranoia: the misguided exclusion on the "Ellis Island of the West," Angel Island.

Up and down the West Coast, too, thousands travelled in steamers initially taken off the Panama route and, later, in larger, more commodious craft specially built for the trade, such as the *Columbia, Pomona, Yale, Santa Rosa* and *Harvard*. Steam schooners, built to replace the sailing schooners in the lumber trade, also carried passengers in ships like *Wapama, Multnomah, Klamath* and *Pomo*. On the inland waters, particularly for the riverboat routes that pierced California's heartland and led passengers from San Francisco to inland ports including Stockton and Sacramento, magnificent vessels were built that rivaled the opulence of the Mississippi River steamboats. It was a tribute of sorts that after the retirement of one of the last and greatest California riverboats, the *Delta Queen,* she was towed to the Gulf to be "restored" in the best Mark Twain style to the Mississippi riverboat she never was. On San Francisco Bay, ferryboats large and small plied between Sausalito, Oakland and other ports to San Francisco. Vessels like the *Eureka, Encinal, Berkeley, James M. Donahue* and *San Jose* became a part of the city's lore and legendry along with a prominent San Francisco landmark, the Ferry Building. Sharing the Bay with the ferries were smaller craft, which performed a variety of valuable services. These included fishing craft ranging from the junks of numerous Chinese fishermen to the feluccas of Mediterranean immigrants. They also included the small, shallow-draft scow schooners, workhorses of the bay like *Alma* and *Charles W.,* which numbered more than 500 and brought small but vital cargoes of produce, hay and fertilizer from farms and ranches situated on the shallow sloughs and deltas of the Bay.

On shore, the city also had a rich and varied collection of maritime businesses and establishments. Piers, docks, wharves and landings dominated the entire San Francisco waterfront and were served by a shore-side railroad, the Belt Line, which had been constructed just for that purpose. Ship chandlers, shipping agents, pilots and boatmen were a part of the waterfront, along with the usual collection of bars, brothels and boardinghouses of "sailortown" and the Barbary Coast. Marine lookouts atop Telegraph Hill and Point Lobos, and later on piers jutting out into the Bay, spotted incoming ships, as did the lookouts at smaller, more hidden sites that served a progression of mighty seacoast fortifications. These ranged from earthworks with smoothbore cannon to massive underground concrete casemates housing naval guns capable of firing 20 miles out to sea. Fourteen lighthouses on San Francisco Bay and at the Golden Gate guided mariners, along with fog signals. The first lighthouse on the Pacific coast was built on Alcatraz Island in 1854; the first fog signal on the Pacific coast was installed at Point Bonita, just outside the Bay, in 1856. Two lifesaving stations adjacent to the lights at Fort Point and Point Bonita and two stations at Ocean Beach on the city's western shore aided mariners in distress; hundreds of vessels ran aground, foundered or capsized in or near the harbor. Other vessels made their maiden plunge from shipyards around the Bay, which launched everything from the smallest wooden scow schooner to warships and the gigantic steel liberty ships of World War II, such as *Jeremiah O'Brien, Benjamin Warner, William A. Richardson* and *Robert E. Peary.*

Great moments in American maritime history transpired in San Francisco, from the refinement and naming of the "art" of shanghaiing to the establishment of the Coast Seaman's Union (later rechristened the Sailor's Union of the Pacific), which was the first effective American sailor's union. The still widely remembered and controversial longshoreman's strike of 1934 took place on the San Francisco waterfront. Most important, though, was the work of Sailor's Union leader Andrew Furuseth, whose lobbying bettered the lot of the American seaman through laws banning corporal punishment and shipboard brutality. Great disasters, such as the sinking of the liner *City of Rio de Janeiro* off Fort Point in 1901 with a loss of more than 100 lives, and the ramming and sinking of the Korean War hospital ship *Benevolence* in 1950 with a loss of 23 lives, have occurred at the city's doorstep. Likewise great heroism has occurred on the Bay, such as that of John Napoli, an Italian fisherman who saved some 70 lives after the *Benevolence* sank, jettisoning his cargo and sustaining a permanently disabling back injury while he pulled drowning crewmembers from the cold sea.

These elements and many, many more combined to create the maritime tradition of San Francisco. It is a tradition rich in history, action, and the careers of the thousands of ships that sailed to and from San Francisco. It is also a tradition tied to the lives of hundreds of thousands of sailors, shoreside merchants and workers, and to the residents of the city by the sea where, in the words of poet George Sterling, "At the end of our streets are spars/Slender spars in the offing, Mast and Yard in the slips/How they tell on the azure/Of the sea-contending ships!" But though this tradition remained in memory—in the reminiscences of mates, masters, owners and the regular Jack Tar as well as in such works of literature as Jack London's stories and Peter B. Kyne's Cappy Ricks sagas—eventually it began to fade, slipping away as the port declined in importance. And then many of the old ships were wrecked, left to rot in stagnant backwaters, burned for their metal fastenings or towed away to suffer ignominious dismemberment in shipbreaker's yards.

Interest in San Francisco's maritime past always existed in some quarters, and the first efforts at saving a part of it for public appreciation dates to short-lived and at times misguided displays such as that of the *Success,* an 1840s ship that at one point had served as a floating jail in Melbourne harbor and was brought to San Francisco during the Panama Pacific International Exposition of 1915 to be exhibited as "the Convict Ship." There were also small displays of ship models and paintings at the M. H. de Young Museum in Golden Gate Park and at the Golden Gate International Exposition of 1939. These well-intended efforts fell short of preserving a living part of the city's seafaring past. In the 1940s, though, a few young maritime enthusiasts, armed with little more than a dream, perseverance, and the realization that San Francisco's maritime tradition would soon be irretrievably lost, began to work for the preservation of that tradition. It was then that Karl Kortum, Harry Dring, David Nelson, Scott Newhall and others were joined by civic leaders in creating a protected enclave of the city's maritime past.

The concept of saving a historic ship was not exactly new in San Francisco. In 1909 Roald Amundsen beached his ship *Gjoa,* the first vessel to successfully navigate the Northwest Passage, on San Francisco's Ocean Beach. *Gjoa* remained in San Francisco, in a rock and sand berth, slowly rotting away until finally returned to Norway six decades later. The *Gjoa* had not moved the city to preserve any of its past, let alone the ship. The passing of the tall ships and the decline of the port had seemingly stifled the city's ties to the ships that had made her great. But when the first of San Francisco's living museum ships—the 1886 square-rigger rechristened *Balclutha*—was triumphantly and lovingly brought back from the dead through the efforts of

the museum, maritime unions, and thousands of hours of volunteer labor by scores of sailors, shipyard employees, and enthusiasts, she marked the rekindling of a maritime spirit in San Francisco.

The success of *Balclutha* in turn sparked new endeavors. Working with the San Francisco Maritime Museum, historians and progressive state legislators along with officials of California's Division of Beaches and Parks began to assemble a new, innovative state historic park on the San Francisco waterfront. At Hyde Street Pier (once the San Francisco landing for the ferries of Southern Pacific Golden Gate Ferries Limited), a collection of characteristic West Coast vessels, some of them the last of their types, were gathered with the advice and support of the maritime museum to create the San Francisco Maritime State Historic Park. Informally known as the San Francisco Historic Ships, the vessels moored at Hyde Street Pier grew in number from the earliest acquisitions of the mid-1950s to include the three-masted lumber schooner *C. A. Thayer* (1895), the steam schooner *Wapama* (1915), the ferry *Eureka* (formerly known as *Ukiab,* dating from 1890), the scow schooner *Alma* (1891) and the steam tugboat *Hercules* (1907). A theme park somewhat similar to Connecticut's Mystic Seaport had been envisioned, with small boats, buildings and large nautical artifacts displayed outdoors. Small boats were collected, outdoor exhibits were placed on the pier, and two structures—the late-19th-century office of the Tubbs Cordage Company, first firm to commercially manufacture rope on the West Coast, and a houseboat, the Lewis Ark—were restored and relocated on the pier. In 1970 the pilothouse of the boat *George Shima* was placed on the pier; it was joined in 1975 by the pilothouse of the tug *Sea Fox* to serve as office space for the state park staff.

Earlier and larger development plans drafted by the San Francisco Maritime Museum had called for a major museum complex. Dubbed Project X, the plan had grown out of the dreams of Karl Kortum, who had become museum curator. Wanting to preserve the flavor of the old waterfront, Kortum envisioned the preservation of nearby brick warehouses, the extension of the Hyde Street cable-car line to the pier, the development of a Victorian-era public park and the establishment of a major state railroad museum. Additional historic ships would join those already moored in the lagoon of Aquatic Park off Hyde Street Pier. Hemmed in on all sides by the railroad museum, Victorian park and the San Francisco Maritime Museum, the expanded facility would not only take after but rival Mystic Seaport. Among the significant gains made were the extension of the cable-car line, the development of Victorian Park, the acquisition of one of the warehouses (the Haslett Warehouse) and the preserva-tion of the other surrounding warehouses as private developers threw their resources behind the renovation of the dilapidated waterfront, an effort that culminated ultimately in the development of Ghirardelli Square, The Cannery and Fisherman's Wharf as major tourist attractions. Yet the plan did not completely succeed.

Project X mired down in a morass of infighting, lack of funds, legal problems and the incessant need of the ships for constant and diligent care. The trite adage that ships are holes in the water, lined with wood, into which money is poured was found to be true. Project X, after a fair start, died away without a forest of masts moored in the Aquatic Park lagoon, and the Haslett Warehouse, site of the projected railroad museum, was partially redeveloped as revenue-generating office space. Even worse, the ships continued to physically deteriorate as a limited state budget was strained to maintain them. The creation of a major new public park entity, the National Park Service's Golden Gate National Recreation Area, finally plotted a new course for the historic ships and the San Francisco Maritime Museum. In 1977 the San Francisco Maritime State Historic Park was transferred to the National Park Service. This transfer was followed by that of the San Francisco Maritime Museum in 1978 and *Balclutha* in 1979. Some of the hard-working people who had done so much to preserve the dream of the historic ships—Karl Kortum, Harry Dring and Harlan Soeten—also joined the National Park Service to work toward a major, national maritime museum. Entrusted now with the fruit of the hard labor of many and one of the gems of the state park system, the Golden Gate National Recreation Area was faced with a tremendous challenge. The San Francisco Maritime Museum and the Maritime State Historic Park were combined to create one entity, the National Maritime Museum of San Francisco. The National Park Service constructed a new, professional storage facility to house thousands of artifacts, paintings and ship fittings not on display, and in mid-1983 a new, expanded library of books, records, blueprints and logbooks from the old Maritime Museum was opened in new, spacious quarters.

The National Park Service also inaugurated a program of maritime archaeological work. Maritime archaeology had inauspiciously begun in San Francisco in 1978 when the 1835 ship _Niantic,_ beached, burned and buried beneath encroaching landfill on the San Francisco waterfront during the gold rush, was found during highrise construction, her hold still packed with merchandise stored there by argonaut merchants. A lack of funding and the need for continued construction led to the destruction of the _Niantic_ despite the best efforts of many, including the developer, the San Francisco Maritime Museum and committed volunteers. Phoenixlike, however, a strong professional commitment to archaeological excavation and preservation followed, largely spearheaded by the late Roger Olmsted and his wife Nancy. Olmsted, who had worked as a member of the San Francisco Maritime Museum staff in years past, had greatly contributed to the museum and the historic ships' preservation and interpretation. In his work with archaeologist Allen Pastron and naval architect Ray Aker, Olmsted revealed previously unknown and significant maritime treasures buried beneath the city's streets: the nearly complete remains of the 1840 whaler _Lydia_ and the most intact remains of a San Francisco gold rush ship yet found, a hulk believed to be the ship _William Gray,_ which was built around 1825 and disappeared in bay fill sometime after 1852. Following Olmsted's lead since his unexpected death in 1981, National Park Service historians, archaeologists and anthropologists are working to retrieve important historical and archaeological data from the hulls of wrecked ships, many of which lie within the boundaries of the Golden Gate National Recreation Area. Work done between 1980 and 1983 has revealed the remains of the Pacific Mail steamer _Tennessee,_ the 1882 lumber schooner _Neptune,_ the 1903 steam schooner _Pomo,_ the 1919 freighter _Munleon_ and the nearly intact hull of the 1856 ship _King Philip._

The Golden Gate National Recreation Area has also pursued acquisition of other historic vessels. In 1979 the steam paddle tug *Eppleton Hall* was donated by the National Maritime Museum Association. The National Park Service is also currently considering an offer from a group of private investors to acquire on loan the riverboat *Delta King,* which would be moored with the historic ships to serve as a private residential vessel with public access to museum spaces on board. Despite the many positive achievements of the National Park Service's tenure, the historic ships are still plagued with problems, many of which date from their earliest years in the Maritime State Historic Park. The need for constant maintenance, the lack of money and a plethora of preservation problems have created a serious and compelling need for immediate action, or the ships will be lost. It is not that the National Park Service does not care about the precious resources entrusted to its care. According to recently retired National Park Service Assistant Director for Cultural Resources Francis Ross Holland, Jr., himself a respected maritime historian,

> There is no question the Service is committed to the preservation and interpretation of this country's maritime heritage. The question is how well we will be permitted to perform this work. . . . The fact is that while the National Park system has expanded greatly in the past few years, the administration and the Congress have been cutting back on funds and personnel. . . . Progress in the maritime field is slow, unfortunately, because of fiscal and personnel restraints imposed upon us.

The plight of the ships and the National Park Service is best summarized in the case of *Wapama. Wapama,* last of her kind and sole representative of all of America's wooden passenger- and freight-carrying steamers, is rotting away in a backwater of the Oakland Estuary, reposing, undignified, on a barge the National Park Service placed her on in 1979 when structural damage that conceivably could have snapped her in half was detected in her keel. The hope was that $2 million to restore the ship would be forthcoming—but it was not. Now, five years later, *Wapama,* since designated a nationally significant vessel, still rests out of the water, the cost of her preservation doubled due to inflation and rot incurred by being out of the water for so long. Help is on the way with Congressional appropriations and the never-ceasing concern of *Wapama* aficionados. However the sad fact is that *Wapama* was almost over the brink, with plans of scuttling at sea, a blazing funeral pyre, or ignominious dismantling, before the rallying cry was heard.

As the 20th century draws to a close, the innovative dream of the historic ships must be reaffirmed. A challenge has been issued by the generation that

From her berth, Pampanito has a bird's-eye periscope view of San Francisco.

saved the ships and by the preceding generation as well—those who built, sailed, and sometimes died in the ships. The challenge is to save them once again and to maintain them in a proud, shipshape fashion with decks clean, rigging tight, hulls sound and occasionally with their canvas spread and steam up, so that our children and our children's children can tread the decks, smell the salt air, feel the ocean swell beneath their feet and experience firsthand the ships that created San Francisco and carried us so far.

James P. Delgado
National Park Service

Preface

*T*HERE'S AN OLD SAYING that identifies the three most beautiful things in the world as a woman with child, a full moon and a full-rigged ship. No one knows who first linked the three images, but chances are it was a deepwater seaman aboard a mighty windjammer scudding toward some distant port like Rangoon or Iquique. For most of us today, it's hard to imagine the soulful experience of sailing aboard the great ships of the past. What did deepwatermen see and hear during their long voyages? Just how strong was the smell aboard a cod-fishing sailing schooner? How back-breaking was the work aboard a lumber schooner? Who filled the cramped holds of these ships, and why did they go to sea?

This book supplies answers to these and other questions by looking at San Francisco's historic ships. Eight vessels have been restored to their original splendor and are docked along the city's north waterfront in the Golden Gate National Recreation Area. It's a renowned collection; in terms of gross tonnage of historical craft it's the largest in the world. Nearby you'll find the National Maritime Museum, a repository of rare artifacts, ship models, and library materials (including photographs), the West Coast center of maritime historical research.

The book focuses mainly on the five historic ships you can board and tour: the square-rigger *Balclutha*, sailing schooner *C. A. Thayer*, ferryboat *Eureka*, liberty ship *Jeremiah O'Brien* and World War II submarine *Pampanito*. It begins with an account of the citywide intrigue leading to the establishment of the Maritime Museum and acquisition of *Balclutha*. In the late 1940s, ship lovers banded together to cajole newspaper editors, shipping magnates and finally San Francisco City Hall into supporting a drive to preserve the maritime lore of the West Coast. Their success spurred them to pursue an even more daring dream: purchase and restoration of one of the last great square-rigged ships, *Balclutha*. The anecdotal stories you find here about life aboard the ships together with a walk along their decks will help put you in touch with the sailing experience of an earlier day.

14

The wooden duchess looks on while a shipfitter cuts away the bobstay with an acetylene torch prior to removing the outer end of the spike bowsprit.

One vessel closed to public tours has managed to work its way into these pages. *Alma,* the little scow schooner, is representative of a type of craft so vital to the growth of the entire Bay Area that to omit her would be to leave the historical picture incomplete.

Two ships also docked at the Hyde Street Pier, the steam tug *Hercules* and the paddle-wheel tug *Eppleton Hall,* are not lengthily discussed here. This is not meant in any way to diminish their importance historically. *Hercules* is an ocean-going steam tug with a huge, 1000-horsepower triple-expansion engine. She represents the best of the American-built ocean-going steam tugs and is one of the last of her kind still afloat in North America. *Eppleton Hall*'s origins reach across the Atlantic to the Wear and Tyne rivers in England, where she worked from 1914 until she was sold for scrap in 1968. *San Francisco Chronicle* editor Scott Newhall then salvaged her and sailed her from Newcastle upon Tyne to San Francisco, 11,000 miles in a 105-foot paddle-wheel tug; she too is the last of her kind. (Newhall's adventures are recorded in his book *The Eppleton Hall.*) You can't board the tugs, but you can view them from the Hyde Street Pier.

Maintaining all the historic ships is a formidable responsibility for the National Park Service. The vessels require periodic dry-docking for inspection, cleaning and repair; their unique characteris-

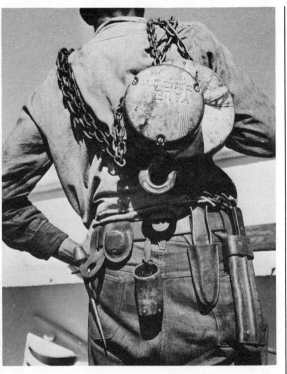

Rigger's belt with tools: heavy knife (from right), pliers, tallow horn, and pricker. A modern chain tackle is slung over the shoulder.

15

tics often call for hard-to-find materials, such as special timbers that can take up to six months to acquire. Finding men with old-fashioned shipwright skills to repair the vessels is a troubling problem in itself.

A craftsman carves the scrollwork on C. A. Thayer's stemhead.

But by far the greatest obstacle to efficient maintenance is the scarcity of money available for ship preservation. All the ships (except *Pampanito,* which is owned and managed by the National Maritime Museum Association) must compete for funding with a large number of other National Park Service projects. Still, the required funds are usually scraped together; after all, almost every ship in the collection is enrolled on the National Register of Historic Places.

Despite the ships' national historic status, however, near-ruinous delays in funding do occur. The latest and most serious case involves the steam schooner *Wapama* (whose role in the West Coast lumber trade is discussed in the chapter on the *C. A. Thayer*). Her troubles began in 1979 when she was removed from the Hyde Street Pier for drydock repairs in Oakland. She had been a popular attraction; for 16 years children and adults had delighted in wandering the decks of this wooden-hulled steam lumber schooner, the last of her kind. But by the time she reached the dry dock in Oakland, the estimated $1.2 million needed to repair dry rot within her hull was nowhere to be found. There was a series of delays, and *Wapama*'s condition worsened, her hull nearing the cracking point. A variety of imaginative funding plans were worked up by those close to her, but none succeeded. By the beginning of 1983 not a penny had been spent on her repair and the total cost of saving her had risen to $4.8 million. Then in February 1983 the National Park Service announced a three- to five-year plan to restore *Wapama,* deriving funds from several sources. This is a hopeful sign, and if the plan succeeds *Wapama* will reclaim her rightful place among the significant historic ships at the Hyde Street Pier.

1. Creation of the Maritime Museum and Acquisition of Balclutha

ALL EYES FOCUSED ON CLAR-ENCE LINDNER, publisher of the *San Francisco Examiner*. Lunch at the posh Bohemian Club was winding down, and it was time for a decision. Would he join the city's other newspaper executives and throw his weight behind a proposed maritime museum for San Francisco?

No one was more eager for his support than a top *Chronicle* editor named Scott Newhall, who had assembled the publishers on this overcast Friday in September 1949. He had taken on the museum drive six months before as a personal crusade. Now the entire project seemed to hang in the balance.

Lindner had already written once to Newhall rejecting the plan outright, favoring instead a port project. "Money, brains and effort of the community should go toward bringing the port back into shape before that passes into history," the *Examiner* chief said. But Newhall knew what lay at the root of Lindner's opposition. Mrs. Alma de Brettville Spreckels, contentious wife of the late sugar baron Adolph Spreckels, had written to the publisher to promote her own Museum of Science and Industry, an institution she was struggling to launch; few people had heard of it, no one had seen it. Yet Mrs. Spreckels asked for support in locating a place to house her maritime collection of artifacts

Tugs escort Balclutha *under the Bay Bridge in 1955 to her new berth at Fisherman's Wharf.*

and ship models. Lindner mistook her efforts for those Newhall was spearheading. "Additionally," he wrote, "my friend Mrs. Spreckels seems to have taken over the project. Her letter to sundry citizens indicates you are her 'appanage' in it. I am cool to her promotion of a Museum of Science and Industry, and don't feel like putting time, effort and money into this one."

To succeed, the project needed the backing of all four San Francisco newspapers; there was no room for carping and divisiveness. With a united front, Newhall figured, the proposal would blow like a juggernaut up the steps of City Hall, where the mayor would offer his stamp of approval or face a scolding in the press.

After failing to reach Lindner by phone for two days, Newhall hired a courier to deliver a written clarification to the publisher's door. His letter began on a note of frustration—"I am very disappointed that you are not warmer toward this project at this time"—and moved on to outline the plan, emphasizing its historical significance for San Francisco and the opportunity for national publicity, tourist appeal and civic unity. "This project is for San Francisco," Newhall wrote, "and needs the participation of a great many people. Mrs. Spreckels should certainly be one of those people." But she was not going to dominate, Newhall assured. "We want this to be a community project, and not the special platform of the *Chronicle,* or of Mrs. Spreckels, or of anyone else." In closing, Newhall asked Lindner to join the other publishers for lunch the following day. Lindner telephoned to accept, saying inscrutably "I'll be at the luncheon, kid" and abruptly hanging up.

Getting Lindner to attend was one thing; getting his vote was quite another. Over lunch, Lindner revived the issue of Mrs. Spreckels and her Museum of Science and Industry. He dismissed her entire collection as "a pile of crap," at which point Newhall leapt in to reaffirm the strict limitations to be imposed on Mrs. Spreckels' influence. This was not to be a tea-drinking social society but a serious institution dedicated to maritime history and scholarship.

Newhall's two young workhorses, the men whose legwork had brought the project this far, presented the plan in detail. Karl Kortum, an imaginative Petaluma country boy with a passion for ships, described the proposed exhibits for the Maritime Museum and pointed out where and how a collection of restored historic ships was to be docked nearby at Aquatic Park. David Nelson, a quick-witted *Chronicle* reporter with political savvy gained from studies at the Coro Foundation, explained the plan's schedule and required costs and personnel. As a team, the two young men were an ideal match, their skills dovetailing. Kortum was a

21

born strategist; he dreamed and plotted on a grand scale, but he was rather slow on his feet and sometimes gruff and stubborn. Nelson was a natural tactician, likable and confident, possessing an exceptional ability to weave successfully through the labyrinths of city hall and business. At the *Chronicle* offices, before Nelson set off on his appointed rounds of the influential, the two would simulate likely encounters, with Kortum playing the unbending politician or corporate executive and Nelson as himself struggling to bring the reluctant into line. The exercise helped Nelson to anticipate some tough questions and to have cogent responses at hand. Such preparation and dynamic execution induced state park commissioners, shipping leaders, waterfront union bosses and wealthy patrons to lend their names and prestige to the project by signing on to the museum's board of trustees. To add the promise of success, only one city newspaper still needed to be wooed.

As the luncheon meeting drew to a close the time arrived for a roll call, the moment of reckoning. As expected, voices of approval came from Joe Cauthorn, publisher of the *San Francisco Daily News,* Randolph Hearst, of the *Call-Bulletin,* and Newhall, who represented Paul Smith, publisher of the *Chronicle.* There was nothing more to be said; the others waited on Lindner, and when he opened his mouth it was to announce that the city's newspapers were from that moment unanimous. "I looked around this charming little room," Kortum noted in his diary, "and realized that the neglected old windjammers were going to finally have their day—we were past the last hurdle." But the euphoria was fleeting. "Back at the office," he added, "there was a relaxed, almost letdown feeling. We had done it, but were too enmeshed in the techniques of the fight to really realize it."

For Karl Kortum the fight had begun more than a decade before. As early as 1937, at age 20, Kortum was pushing for historic ship preservation. He noted in his diary on July 19, 1937 that the organizers of the 1939 Golden Gate International Exposition on Treasure Island ought to restore the downeaster *St. Paul* and set her up as an exhibition. He even went so far as to write a six-page exhortation to the fair's director. When he visited the exposition's maritime exhibit in 1939, however, he found only a display of ship models and went home

sadly disappointed. On March 1, 1939 he confided to his diary:

> My idea for an exposition here would be less plaster and land structures and instead a lagoon running into the heart of the island with a dozen historic ship types anchored in San Francisco Bay with scow schooners running expeditions in amongst the mighty windships, and each day the majestic ceremony of a little paddle wheel tug passing her line aboard a different ship, the crew manning the capstan with a chantey sung out (by broadcast) across the waters, the anchor slowly rising to the hawse pipe and the ship getting under way and being towed in to a replica of a picturesque old "Frisco dock."

An extravagant dream, perhaps; born of the writer's youthful exuberance. But it contained the seed of what was to become a reality along San Francisco's north waterfront. Today, there are indeed the mighty windships docked along the pier; there is a scow schooner as well, and even a little paddle-wheel tug.

Kortum waited nearly ten years before launching a serious campaign. It had occurred to him that his imagined lagoon already existed at Aquatic Park, and nearby on shore was a marvelous three-story WPA structure built as a fun house and casino but perfectly suited for use as a museum. Certainly, the lagoon needed only a few proud windjammers and the abandoned casino a few ship models and paintings to revitalize the entire Aquatic Park area.

It was in order to convey this notion that Kortum landed on the doorstep of the Spreckels mansion in 1948. He had roped his buddy Jimmy Walpole into coming along, and between the two of them they'd get inside and fill Mrs. Spreckels' ear with the romance of a maritime park. Walpole and Kortum had sailed together aboard the bark *Kaiulani,* rounding Cape Horn with a cargo of lumber in 1941. Walpole's easy, winning style would get them through the door; "he was the nicest, most amiable man I ever met in my life," Kortum remembers. And Kortum's nautical expertise would take over from there.

Mrs. Spreckels had been chosen because of her demonstrated interest in establishing a maritime museum. There had been safeguarding efforts, however, preceding hers. In 1925, Edward S. Clark and William F. Breeze, devoted scholars and collectors, founded the Pacific Model Society to encourage preservation of Pacific Coast maritime lore.

By the middle of the 1930s the organization had become the Pacific Marine Research Society and had expanded to embrace all historical maritime matters. Its members included David Dickie, of the famous local shipbuilding family; Henry Rusk, marine artist and curator at the de Young Museum; Bill Muir, scion of the shipsmith firm Muir & Simon; and J. Porter Shaw, collector and marine antiquarian, whose name would later be attached to the maritime museum's library.

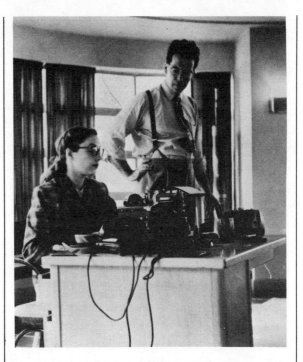

In early days, Kortum and his wife, Jean, were the only staff members. Now there are more than fifty.

The young Kortum and his friend Jack Eatherton used to hitchhike from Petaluma to attend the society's meetings at the Bellevue Hotel and El Jardin restaurant. Harry Dring, who was to become a noted ship preservationist and the driving force behind the rescue of the steam tug *Hercules,* used to buzz over from Oakland on his motorcycle.

Bill Dodge (right), who organized the volunteer rigging gang, lays aloft on the topmast shrouds with Chandler Raymond (center) and Johnny Grueland.

Edward Clark's persistence with the project was partially rewarded in 1939 when he was asked to assemble a maritime exhibit for the Golden Gate International Exposition on Treasure Island. Clark responded by persuading local collectors and steamship companies to provide ship models and artifacts. Later, he invited Mrs. Spreckels out to Treasure Island to see the exhibit; it sparked her enthusiasm and she began to take over the museum drive. She paid the bills for removing the collection when the exposition ended and kept many of the pieces together. In time, Clark was eased out, and Mrs. Spreckels invented her letterhead organization, the Museum of Science and Industry.

Relying on the grande dame's growing commitment, Kortum punched the front doorbell of her mansion. A mechanical buzzing noise then prompted Walpole to shove the door open, causing daylight to slant into a broad, funereal hallway. The men tiptoed forward like a pair of second-story men, Walpole's shirttail straying below the lining of his sports jacket. At the far end was a sight to widen Kortum's farm-boy eyes; here was something he had never seen in someone's home: a private elevator.

They rode to the second floor, where they were intercepted by Jean Scott Frickelton, Mrs. Spreckels' paid companion and publicist. She made no attempt to conceal her alarm and interrogated fiercely: Who were they? What did they want? Didn't they know this was a private residence? Jimmy Walpole fielded the inquiries like a campaigning congressman. Gradually the flush left the woman's face and she consented to escort them to the Italian Room, where they'd find Mrs. Spreckels. "For second-story men," Kortum chuckled, reminiscing years later, "I guess promoting a square-rigged ship and a maritime museum sounded like an unusual line."

In the Italian Room, Mrs. Spreckels, nearing 70, sat upright with the comforts of her day-to-day life arranged before her; they included the telephone, her address book, several sharpened pencils and a writing tablet, assorted pills—red ones, blue ones, green ones—and within arm's reach a pitcher of martinis. She wore a black wrapper with a white feather boa draped around her neck. A diamond brooch sparkled at her breast like an exploding star. She looked every bit the grande dame propped up on her throne of red velour. But on her feet in roguish contrast were a pair of five-and-dime fuzzy-wuzzy bedroom slippers.

The Italian Room itself was like a venerable reading room: high carved ceiling, gaping fireplace. Against one wall stood two life-size statues of Nubian slaves brandishing spears; they were collared and chained to the wall. A grand piano decorated one corner but seemed shrunken, toylike, in the sweeping breadth of the room.

The character of Mrs. Alma Emma Le Normand de Bretteville Spreckels was as streaked with contradiction as the dime store slippers might suggest. At one moment she was the great philanthropist donating millions of dollars for a memorial to 3600 Californians who died in World War I; and her California Palace of the Legion of Honor is a splendid San Francisco treasure. At the next instant, however, she would arch her back and snarl when, for example, museum employees asked for $50 to buy baseball uniforms to join a local league. "Fifty dollars! Where do you expect me to get $50?" she was reported to have said. "You people have my skin. Now you want my guts!" As a youngster, she had had formal art training, even accepting an offer to pose for the statue of Victory that crowns the Spanish American war monument in Union Square. She was a California native but clung to her French ancestry, traced back to the French Revolution and Charlotte Corday, who murdered Marat in his bath.

Her importance as one of the founders of the Maritime Museum is undisputed; she joins Edward Clark, Kortum, Newhall and Nelson in that distinction. But the controversy over her character persists to this day. According to David Nelson, the one-time *Chronicle* reporter whose own role was instrumental, Mrs. Spreckels "was a strong-willed old lady who didn't like to be pushed around. Within her capability, within her understanding of how to help, she gave everything she had. A wonderful, wonderful regal lady." Kortum's view is less flattering. "She thought of herself as a character and a card," he said. "She grew up in the artistic society early in the century where people were unconventional and bohemian. A fairly statuesque babe. Her father was a machinist with the Fulton Iron Works. Adolph Spreckels, an heir to the sugar fortune, married her and from that point forward she had

A painter renders a deteriorated Balclutha *onto canvas at a time when she was run up on the Sausalito mud flats the year before the museum bought her.*

money. But she was stingy. She had millions and you had to struggle to get $500 to buy a ship model."

At the time Kortum first faced Mrs. Spreckels, he had no idea what to expect. She listened attentively as he delivered his pitch. He had refined his concept into a standard proposal: use the Aquatic Park casino as a maritime museum and float the square-rigger *Star of Alaska,* originally known as *Balclu-*

tha, in the lagoon outside the casino's back door. Mrs. Spreckels showed stirrings of enthusiasm toward the idea of a museum but closed her ears entirely to the historic ship. To Kortum's mind, ship preservation formed the basis of the entire project. He intensified his bid, insisting he didn't want to create just another maritime museum but something different, something truly distinctive that would show the world San Francisco's great contribution to the history of the seven seas. The best approach, he concluded, was to float that square-rigger in the lagoon for everyone to see.

Kortum's rhetoric was to no avail. Something about the *Star of Alaska* had turned Mrs. Spreckels cold; she tired of listening and shortly Kortum and Walpole found themselves out on the street again. It was the start of a seven-year battle that pitched Mrs. Spreckels in direct opposition to *Balclutha.*

Kortum's next move was to fire off a letter to the mayor, this time enclosing a watercolor rendition of the proposed design for Aquatic Park painted by his Petaluma friend, Frank Eatherton. Mayor Elmer Robinson graciously replied that no city funds were available and referred the letter to the park commission.

Private entreaties apparently carried little weight. What the project needed was to rouse public attention. It was at this point that Kortum turned to Scott Newhall, the only man he knew who was in a position to spread the word. Newhall was editor of the *Chronicle*'s "This World" section and a particularly good bet. He had a keen interest in sailing, had even attempted an around-the-world voyage in a 42-foot ketch. The expedition had to be cut short, however, because skipper Newhall contracted a serious leg infection in Acapulco. He eventually lost the leg but none of his wanderlust. In 1970 he beat tremendous odds by successfully sailing the world's last paddle-wheel tug, the *Eppleton Hall,* from Newcastle upon Tyne in England to San Francisco. (The tug has taken its place among the fleet of historic ships at the Hyde Street Pier.) Kortum's petition could lean on a family connection as well. Newhall's brother, Hall, had sailed with Kortum in 1941 aboard the *Kaiulani* on that last voyage of an American-built square-rigger around Cape Horn.

The entreaty Kortum penned on March 5, 1949 elicited enthusiasm far greater than he had ever expected; in fact, it altered the course of his life and launched his career. He first thanked the *Chronicle* for its help in defeating a proposed freeway through the Kortum farm, then moved on to the meat of his message. Kortum praised Newhall's recent review of a new book by Alan Villiers, adding: "it led me to think that you and the *Chronicle* might be interested in a project of waking San Francisco up to its sailing ship tradition that has haunted me for some ten years. Unless I am mistaken, it is the stuff whereof a good newspaper campaign is made, and which, conversely needs a newspaper campaign — to put it over. The end result would be something to remind the city in very graphic fashion of how far-sighted your paper is, and it would continue to do so as the years roll by." The plan Kortum delivered in five single-spaced pages, an eloquent plea from the heart, served as the basis of what eventually came to life. He continued:

At the foot of Van Ness Avenue is one of the most pointless areas in San Francisco — Aquatic Park — and my proposal is to give it point by concentrating there the story of the city's great maritime past. At the present time the place has motif but no substance; it always reminds me of an empty stage. Well, the star of this show would be a full rigged ship out of San Francisco's past, yards braced square, black topsides, red boot topping. She would be moored to that little pier that curves out into the bay in front of the Aqua-

28

Maritime Museum opening day, May 28, 1951 — the mayor drove up to the speaker's platform aboard an ancient Virginia & Truckee locomotive.

tic Park casino and for a backdrop would have the bay itself, with steamships coming and going from the Golden Gate, and behind that again the full beauty of the Marin hills.

The Casino would be used as a marine museum, it is appropriately designed for that, but the square rigger itself would keynote the area. The ship that would fill the bill, in fact, the only full rigged merchant ship on the face of the earth — now that they have scrapped "Calbuco" in Italy — is the "Star of Alaska." She is down in Southern California waters now, and should be brought back home before it is too late. If any ship ever belonged to San Francisco, it is she — for twenty-six years it was the port of registry printed on her counter. . . .

This would be the start. A complete marine museum is sitting out on Treasure Island at the present time, and nobody knows about it, and if they do, they find it difficult to reach through Navy red tape. It is the collection of marine artifacts, models, and paintings made by Mrs. A. B. Spreckels, and contains such things as the twelve foot model of the five mast, full rigged ship "Preussen" made by Eric Swanson, and so perfect that it is more like a ship than a model. The figurehead of the "Davy Crockett" is there (one of the few clipper ship figureheads extant), as well as the fine figure of Mary, Queen of Scots which was originally on the bows of "Kenilworth." Mrs. Spreckels is dissatisfied with a collection like this being pigeon-holed out on the Island, and the public would be, too, if they knew about it. Particularly with a building like the Aquatic Park casino, right at the foot of Van Ness Avenue, lying empty and some two million dollars invested in the area producing no return, whatsoever. . . .

The park commissioners know nothing about ships and can only think in terms of bronze effigies and flower beds. They don't realize that a sailing ship, particularly the real thing, stirs the general public like nothing else. It does not take sailors to appreciate the beauty and romance implicit in a windjammer.

The color of San Francisco, to visitors, is epitomized by cable cars and her position as the city by the sea. And yet I doubt whether there is a duller waterfront — more thoroughly cemented up — in the whole of the United States. Fisherman's Wharf is the only break in the mass of concrete, and it smacks of boats, not ships and long voyages. The type of thing I am suggesting for Aquatic Park is just what the middle-western visitor expects of San Francisco, and I should think a shrine like this to the ships that built San Francisco should provide material for the Chamber of Commerce for years to come. Not to mention its attractiveness to artists and pictorial use that would be made of it for "Come to San Francisco!" ads in the Saturday Evening Post.

Kortum had been reading the *Saturday Evening Post*; in fact, he had been deriving inspiration from it. He interjected that his idea was not entirely original, but a San Francisco adaptation of a plan already implemented in Mystic, Connecticut. The *Saturday Evening Post* had reported on the successful restoration of the whaler *Charles W. Morgan* and training ship *Joseph Conrad*. And what stirred Kortum's imagination was that not only had two

Kortum was in charge of restoration; here he talks with a welder.

30

square-riggers been preserved, but they were floating in a specially created old-time-waterfront setting. Now, if any city should emulate Mystic, Kortum went on:

> it is San Francisco, the port that inspired the building of the Yankee clipper ships, that supported the magnificent "downeast" Cape Horners until the turn of the century, that sent whaling ships to the Arctic, sealing vessels to the Western Pacific, lumber schooners to the South Seas, and which, in the salmon packing fleet,

had the last great gathering of sailing ships on the face of the earth.

Kortum emphasized the need to establish a West Coast institution for the research and study of local shipping history. But the mood had to be casual and open.

> Fortunately, a marine museum is free of the pedantry that sometimes makes other types of museums into institutions by and for experts, with an annoyed public looking in from the outside. At the Aquatic Park building you could muse over the cap iron from the bark "Gatherer," or the wheel from the downeaster "W. F. Babcock" and in a few steps be out on one of the railed balconies of the building looking at the blue waters of the bay where these vessels were once at home. The atmosphere would be of salt water and sea breezes.

He described various ships that might join the fleet and identified figureheads and bow sections for display. He ended on a gloomy note that carried an implied challenge to San Francisco.

> There is a characteristic phrase you keep hearing in San Francisco— "Yes, that came around the Horn in a sailing ship." It irritates me every time I hear it, because it is a reminder that the city by the Golden Gate has thoroughly botched the telling of a great story.

Where Kortum had run up against indifference before, he now won outright approval. His passion and reason sparked something deep within the *Chronicle* editor, but Newhall on his own could go only so far. His immediate task was to interest *Chronicle* publisher Paul Smith; Newhall composed a temperate memo:

> Readers' ideas for civic projects are a nickel a dozen, I realize. Nevertheless, the enclosed letter outlines an idea which fascinates me so I'm taking the liberty of sending it to you for consideration. . . .
>
> It might fit in with your current activities in re-establishing national confidence in San Francisco's waterfront.
>
> The author is a stubborn and an enthusiastic young man. As you can see his one great passion is sailing. If anybody could put the program over he could.
>
> If you were to consider this project seriously I would be glad to contribute any excess energy I might have.

There was no predicting Paul Smith's reaction. He'd been branded brash and cocky by *Time* when he took over as editor-in-chief of the *Chronicle* in 1937. At the time he was only 26—in fact a boy wonder, the youngest editor of a metropolitan daily in the United States. He tried styling the *Chronicle* after *Time* and the *New York Times,* demanding sharper, broader writing and changing its format. He hired Herb Caen, only to watch him defect to the *Examiner* for more pay, taking a mass audience

with him. Caen eventually returned and later wrote affectionately of Smith:

> Paul lived in the grand manner: driver, house-boy, cook, dinner party for 150. . . . He bought suits a dozen at a time, smoked incessantly, ate too little, slept even less, and was the single best drinker I have ever met—straight scotches, one upon the other, and keeping his head while all about him were falling on theirs, face down.

It took ten days, but Newhall's memo was finally returned from the publisher's office. A message scrawled across the bottom read:

Scott—

I would like to talk to this fellow.

P.

Nearly two weeks later, Newhall received another memorandum, this one directing him to "work out a prospectus with Kortum for study and approval." The *Chronicle* was committed; shortly Smith vowed full support and participation.

From the time of Paul Smith's commitment *Chronicle* backing was so steady that, when business called Smith away just before the meeting at the Bohemian Club, Newhall himself was able to represent the paper's position. Following the successful luncheon, Newhall, Kortum and David Nelson made a call on San Francisco Mayor Elmer

Rolf Sollie makes his way up the topmast shrouds to join his mate hanging the lower topsail yard.

Robinson. As Nelson recalls the December meeting, "there wasn't much to say, just: 'As you know, sir, the publishers of the four newspapers in this fair city. . . .' " The mayor rubbed his chin and scratched his head and said it all sounded very interesting; he'd put it on his reading stand and get to it when he could. But it must have slipped in front of the land acquisition papers he was studying, because on December 12, 1949 the *Chronicle* ran a front-page story headlined:

MARITIME MUSEUM—MAYOR SUGGESTS HISTORIC SHIPS BE ENSHRINED HERE

As though the idea came to him one night in his sleep, the mayor kicked off a city-wide campaign and performed dutifully as chief spokesman. The project glided swiftly forward. On December 28 the San Francisco Board of Supervisors passed a resolution calling for a "living" museum at Aquatic Park. January saw the establishment of the San Francisco Maritime Museum Association. At the end of April the newspapers published an artist's rendering of the proposed park, and in September the Museum Association leased the former casino from the city for $1 per year.

A battery of volunteers working day and night for eight months prepared the casino and installed the exhibits; and when the West Coast's first maritime museum opened in May 1951 it was hailed as a great contribution to the city and to the study of maritime history. One figure notable by her absence at the gala opening was Mrs. Spreckels. She had disapproved of Karl Kortum's imaginative display techniques and, hissing that "anchors belong outdoors!" she fled to Europe. She returned late in the summer, observed the museum's success and threw a large press party.

Operating funds trickled in from the donation box, steamship companies, the city, and members of the museum board of directors, including Mrs. Spreckels. Kortum was installed as curator but worked at everything from custodian to publicist. His salary, $150 per month, was donated by Mrs. Spreckels for nine months. It was welcome financial relief. Kortum had been supporting himself for nearly three years on his own savings. Mrs. Spreckels also provided him with free housing, first in her basement and then in the chauffeur's quarters. In January 1952 the city finally found funds to put the curator on the municipal payroll.

Having to scrape for funds made acquisition of the *Star of Alaska* a business imperative. If the vessel could be restored and opened to the public at Fisherman's Wharf, the draw from admission charges would feed museum employees and maintain the displays. Several board members, however, were satisfied with just a maritime museum. Their

Welder — the Bay Area Metal Trade Council swung in behind the restoration project. Volunteer welders showed up every Saturday for a year.

vision did not extend further than the standard mix of ship models and figureheads. Once again, Mrs. Spreckels led opposition to the ship. Perhaps she feared that a steady source of income would diminish her influence. Or maybe she turned her nose up because *Balclutha*'s windswept decks seemed unsuitable as a setting for tasteful social fêtes.

On a practical level, restoring the square-rigger was an expensive venture, perhaps too expensive for the nascent museum. Mrs. Spreckels addressed this concern in a letter to Sidney Walton, president of the museum association:

> If you succeed in acquiring the "Star of Alaska" it is going to cost a great deal of money to rehabilitate it . . . and I think if you give the matter some thought, you may hesitate before taking on another burden such as the "Star of Alaska" unless you have a great sum of money to maintain and advertise it.

Despite her objections, a ship committee was formed and a serious drive to acquire *Star of Alaska* began in 1953. The committee managed to raise $20,000 toward the ship's purchase and was prepared to go as high as $25,000, but since the ship's owner was holding out for $75,000 negotiations proved a bit thorny from the outset.

The ship's enthusiasts were not about to let her get away; she was a windjammer with a proud and glorious past. Launched as the deepwater merchant ship *Balclutha* in 1886, she sailed around Cape Horn 17 times destined for ports at Callao, Iquique and San Francisco; she rounded the Cape of Good Hope on her voyages to Calcutta, Rangoon and Chittagong. Her next career (1899-1902) saw her hauling lumber from the sawmills of Puget Sound to Australia. Then in 1902 she joined the Alaska salmon trade as the *Star of Alaska*. In 1930 she was the last square-rigger in the salmon industry, making her final voyage north to Alaskan fishing waters.

Her working career at an end, the *Star of Alaska* had found herself in 1933 with a new owner, Frank Kissinger, and a new name: *Pacific Queen*. Her complexion had changed too. As one newspaper reported, she was "painted like a circus wagon with a silver hull, brilliant red masts and spars, and a gilt figurehead." Owner Kissinger took the circus motif a step further, installing a 32-pipe calliope on top of the deckhouse. Whatever attention the calliope failed to attract, Kissinger captured with 1000 red, white and blue electric lights strung on high to outline the masts. In this condition *Pacific Queen* toured the West Coast offering visitors a chance to come aboard for 50 cents.

One old salt made sad-eyed by the spectacle was Capt. P.A. McDonald, who remembered "boarding the pathetic old fraud in 1941 when she was ballyhooed as a former convict or pirate ship. I professed complete ignorance while the one-armed keeper lectured to me the meaning of a 'clipper' versus such other ships as the 'Dunsyre' and the 'Moshulu' of which he had photos plastered on the bulkheads." Captain McDonald knew a thing or two about those two large square-riggers, *Dunsyre* and *Moshulu*; he had sailed as master on both. "Since I paid my two bits admission," he continued, "I

Johnny Grueland started out in the volunteer rigging gang; later he became a full-time staff rigger in the Balclutha *crew.*

35

Tex Kissinger, former carnival motorcycle daredevil, negotiates with museum representatives Max Lembke and Walter Taylor in 1952.

her sister ships were meeting their doom as scrap metal and fishing barges. With a retrospective glance, Kortum noted: "I guess we have to thank him with grudging acknowledgment for hanging on to the ship throughout the war and not taking advantage of the high prices for scrap metal, hulls, and anything that smacked of a ship. If he had unloaded at the right time, say about 1941, he might have picked up $35,000 or so. That would have been the high point of his dealings with the ship."

Kissinger did hang on, though his welcome at various ports waned. He tried to interest Hollywood in *Pacific Queen,* basing his pitch on a bit part she had played in *Mutiny on the Bounty* in 1934.

If anyone knew a good show piece, here was the man: Tex Kissinger, as his friends called him, the circus daredevil who at age 16 captured record-book fame by speeding around the inside of a barrel on his motorcycle. No one had done that before. Tex was a dreamer. He had sold oil property and real estate subdivisions, chicken ranches and oil stock. His greatest scam, the one that got away, was to exhibit an embalmed whale on a railroad flatcar. Who wouldn't pay for a look at that? Then, in the early 1930s, while Kissinger prowled the lobby of a hotel as house detective, an old windjammer captain convinced him that the best show property at that time was one of the last-full rigged ships.

wanted to see how far the gullible ones can be fooled and descended into the 'tween decks and was there introduced to the most fearsome looking stuffed scarecrows representing pirates of note. Although I am fairly well read up on the subject and have the best books written upon 'piracy' I again allowed the fellow to go into detail as to the exploits of this or that pirate represented by individual scarecrows. I wept, not for the cowardly highbinders exhibited, but for the poor ship having fallen upon such evil days."

Whatever ignominy Kissinger may have brought to the *Star of Alaska,* his antics saved her life. All

So Tex acquired the *Star of Alaska* and turned her into the pirate ship *Pacific Queen*. In time she was shunted from pier to pier in Long Beach, her most lucrative port; then she was expelled. She came north and was denied a berth at San Francisco. Finally, Kissinger moved her onto the Marin mud flats, her days as an exhibition pirate ship at an end.

Tex and his wife continued to live on board, as they had for nearly 20 years. It was 1952. Kortum, from his office on the museum's third floor, watched the neglected old lady beat back the elements. "The ship was a wreck, with the backstays parting, and thoroughly gone," he observed. "How the sticks stood upright is a mystery, and a tribute to the inherent strength of the masts themselves—nothing else supported them on the mizzen." Traces of her carnival past lurked in the rigging. Kortum lamented: "Almost to the very last of her service to the Kissingers that bloody awful abomination of a wax pirate dummy, hanging by his neck from the foreyards, continued to swing back and forth in the wind, hanging there month after month, year after year and insulting the intelligence of all those who had paid 50 cents to come aboard. I don't know what they expected to see, but the mixture of an old movie ship, an Alaska Packers cannery ship, and a Cape Horner—served up with a thick helping of 'pirate' ship—was about as much as the average sightseer could stand."

Shortly after *Pacific Queen*'s beaching at Sausalito, Tex Kissinger's days came to an end. During a severe storm one night he collapsed and died while inspecting the deck for damage.

The negotiations initiated by the Maritime Museum in 1953 were conducted with the captain's wife, Rose Kissinger. Her original demand of $75,000 was a warning of the headaches to come. Discussion dragged on for a year as the persistent ship committee entreated, flattered, even threatened her. Mrs. Kissinger's price floated high and low but never hovered at the museum's firm limit, $25,000, long enough for a signed agreement. When David Nelson said pointedly that her capriciousness might lose her the sale because very few board members favored the expense anyway, she burst into tears, tore up the written offer in her hand, and stormed from the room screaming "They're highbinders! They're sons of bitches!" Another time she called the newspapers to announce she'd decided to sell *Pacific Queen* to the Navy for use as a target ship outside the Golden Gate.

In desperation, Kortum resorted to scare tactics. He enlisted the aid of a keen negotiator named Captain Leighton Robinson, an 81-year-old deepwaterman who had sailed round the Horn to San Francisco in 1896. Captain Robinson was sent to Mrs. Kissinger with word that the museum was arranging to buy the *Star of India,* an Alaska Packers

After Tex Kissinger died, negotiations for Balclutha *were handled by his wife Rose (right), who was a tough customer. At first she wanted no less than $75,000 for the square-rigger. Captain Leighton Robinson (center), serving as intermediary between Mrs. Kissinger and the museum association, helped secure the vessel for $25,000. Jack Lowe (left), who here entertains Mrs. Kissinger, married her shortly after the* Balclutha *deal was struck.*

bark berthed at San Diego. This was unlikely, although Kortum was "negotiating" with Jerry MacMullen, the *India*'s savior and protecting angel. San Diego was not about to give up her sailing ship treasure.

At the same time, a rift within the museum board itself was undermining the strength of the ship committee. A climax came April 19, 1954, the day of the board's annual meeting. Kortum was determined to head off the opposition; but he needed the backing of Harry Lundeberg, secretary treasurer of the Sailor's Union of the Pacific. Lundeberg was gruff, blunt and probably the most powerful man on the waterfront. He listened to Kortum's plea and grunted that he'd be at the meeting.

Lundeberg arrived at 3:30 P.M. and David Nelson tried to introduce him to two board members, both prominent shipping magnates. Lundeberg just growled "Yeh, I know 'em!" and took his seat. The minor items on the agenda were handled swiftly, then attention turned to the crisis at hand.

Among the more vocal opponents to buying the square-rigger was Capt. T. C. Conwell, an executive at American President Lines. For months he had advocated the ship's purchase, but now he urged that the project be dropped. For a small historical organization *Pacific Queen* might be too great an undertaking, he said. In sheer size, the ship rivalled the museum itself. Once the funds for purchase were secured, the money needed for restoration far exceeded the association's resources.

Conwell's concluding remark, that it was folly to spend so much money on a ship that didn't even have scrap value, brought Lundeberg to his feet. He began softly: "The scrap value is no way to set a price for the last great sailing ship left on the coast." With mounting intensity, he pointed out that *Pacific Queen* was far more than a hulk of steel and wood. She was a banner of spirit, harking back to the city's prosperous maritime past and inspiring greatness for the future. Lundeberg exuded the strength and confidence of a natural leader. By the end of the meeting, his rhetoric had persuaded Conwell to return to the fold; and the board resolved to continue the pursuit of *Pacific Queen*.

Two weeks later Mrs. Kissinger gave in; mostly she feared losing out to another ship like *Star of India*. She agreed to a sale at $25,000, and the contract permitted the museum association to back out if underwater repairs were estimated to exceed $5,000. Bethlehem Shipyards donated dry-docking facilities, and the old windjammer was towed off the mud at Sausalito for a short trip to Oakland.

Kortum recounted the scene at the Oakland shipyard:

> The tugs nudged her in, the dock-master took over, the camera men swarmed. We watched with some tension as the drydock lifted, and more and more of the hull came into sight. Her

40

bilges looked shiny where she had rubbed in
the mud at Sausalito—that looked pretty good.
But we could not get a close look until the surface of the dock emerged. As soon as the water
cleared from the bow end—the stern of the
dock was still awash—we raced down, rubbed
our hands along her bottom, poked at it, peered

at it. She looked fine! Tom Ingersoll, in charge
of the shipyard, came down in a tin hat and gave
her a critical going over. His verdict: a remarkable state of preservation!

Captain Conwell threw himself energetically
into the restoration, cajoling local industry into
donating a variety of supplies. Mario Grossetti,
business agent of Iron Shipbuilders Union Local 9,
steered union after union into the project. By the
time the scarred pirate ship *Pacific Queen* emerged
from the shipyard a year later she sparkled as the
Cape Horner *Balclutha*. Eighteen labor unions had
given 13,000 hours of free labor; 90 Bay Area business firms had kicked in $100,000 in goods and
services. The generous outpouring afforded a thorough revitalization that otherwise would have cost
the Museum Association $250,000. On July 19, 1955
Balclutha was towed to Pier 43 at Fisherman's
Wharf for a festive rechristening.

Not everyone was happy, however. When the
association purchased *Balclutha,* Mrs. Spreckels
went on record as detesting the ship. She stomped
off to Europe ,declaring that "ships are not for
women." Writing more than four years after *Balclutha* opened to the public, Kortum tried to pin-
point the root of Mrs. Spreckels' behavior:

> Part of her resentment of the *Balclutha* is that
> she 'missed the boat' as far as the ship goes—
> she had the first crack at it. She could have taken

41

me up on my suggestion and presented the ship to the city back in 1947. The gift would have been hailed as comparable to the Palace of the Legion of Honor, which was a generous Spreckels contribution to San Francisco. But she didn't and we had to save the ship the hard way.

All the trouble paid off splendidly. *Balclutha* was docked at Fisherman's Wharf to be close to San Francisco's greatest concentration of tourists and in her first 12 months took in $93,000 from admissions. The income freed the association from dependence on precarious financial sources, but, more importantly, paved the way for future ship acquisitions.

2. The Square-Rigger Balclutha

To WALK *BALCLUTHA'S* DECKS is to live her past. Climb into the fo'c'sle and you'll find seamen's oilskins, ditty bags and sea chests from her deepwater days. Peek 'tween decks for a look at charts showing her voyages round the world, panels on the sailor's life at sea, a display of anchors and grapnels. The story continues in the lower hold, the after quarters, the charthouse, the poop and on deck.

With an initial $10,000 for displays, the museum association took great care in making *Balclutha* herself into a museum. The exhibits take you back as far as her origins on the banks of the Clyde River in Scotland. She was launched by Charles Connell and Company of Glasgow, Scotland, in 1886. Her name derives from the old Gaelic *bal* meaning bastion, rock or town, and *clutha* for the Clyde River. In her early years as a merchant ship she had only fleeting contact with San Francisco. On 4 of her 17 voyages around Cape Horn in the 1880s and 1890s she passed through the Golden Gate to deliver wine and spirits, hardware and coal, and to carry away California grain.

It wasn't until 1902 that *Balclutha* made San

Star of Alaska setting sail off the Golden Gate in the early 1920s. A hand on the bowsprit casts the gasket off the outer jib and another sailor on the fore yard overhauls buntlines as the crew sets that sail.

Francisco her home port. In that year she began her career in the Alaska salmon trade, and nearly every spring thereafter until 1930 she sailed out past such notable landmarks as Alcatraz Island, Lime Point and the Cliff House on her way to the icy fishing waters to the north. Her 1904 voyage to Karluk, Kodiak Island, however, did not bode well for the great square-rigger's new career.

When she set sail for the 1904 season the magnificent salmon run was just a month off. In mid-June the great silver horde, as the pack was called, started its annual move from the deep sea toward freshwater rivers and streams where instinct drove them to spawn. Females and their mates battled their way upstream, leaping through rapids, crashing through tides, even climbing vast waterfalls. Nature impelled them to return to the spot of their birth and, if they escaped the rapacity of the fisherman and the sweeping paw of the great brown bear, they tottered to their spawning grounds often with noses bleeding, fins broken and near death from exhaustion.

Balclutha had provisions and cargo for a standard passage. On board were 1,000 tons of supplies for the Karluk canneries and more than 100 people: fishermen, seamen and cannery workers. From mainmast to mizzen the deck was packed with pens containing sheep, cows, pigs and a bull. Looking after the livestock was a seafaring cowboy, a Texan with a long dusty drawl.

There was also on board a young German seaman named Frank Sommer who had jumped ship at a Howard Street pier in 1900 after coming round the Horn on the four-masted bark *Alsterdamm*. In 1965 Sommer, at age 83, recounted his *Balclutha* experience, which began as a routine voyage to Alaska. But as he was to learn, no voyage to Alaska is ever routine. Northern waters can be as treacherous as the notorious squalls around the Horn. In this case, something happened in the dead of night 19 days out of San Francisco, and *Balclutha,* for the only time in her career, failed to deliver her men to the canneries.

Sommer's opportunity to sail came in April when a man entered his boardinghouse seeking crew members for the trip to Kodiak Island. The young German knew little about Alaska—just what he had heard each winter from fishermen returning with fresh tales of perilous seas and the magnificent salmon run. Yet he jumped at the chance. "I was quite anxious to see Alaska," he recalled. "That little adventure spirit, you know." He and a handful of other foreign seamen grabbed their sea bags and in no time found themselves on a ferry steaming across the Bay to the shipyard of the Alaska Packers Association, the largest salmon operator. The company ran 23 canneries in Alaska with a salmon pack worth $5 million a year. About half of the 32 assorted vessels sent north each spring were company owned; the rest, including *Balclutha,*

The Alaska Packers fleet at the foot of Paru Street in Alameda was the last great gathering of square-rigged ships under the American flag. When she was the Star of Alaska, Balclutha *was part of the fleet, seen here in an early 1920s photo.*

owned by Pope and Talbot Lumber Company, were chartered.

The men boarded *Balclutha* in the Oakland Estuary and staked out their bunks in the bow. It wasn't long before a sailor's union representative tracked them down to verify their membership. The union had been formed in the 1880s but didn't gain strength until a successful strike in 1901. Three years later, when Sommer sailed, it was making strides to improve wages and working conditions at sea, proving to be a boon to sailors and fishermen all along the coast.

Balclutha's cannery workers, called the China Gang, arrived the next day. They were of lowest rank in the rigid caste system aboard ship. In the early days of salmon packing, China Gangs were exlusively Chinese; by 1904 Japanese, Filipinos, blacks, Mexicans and a few whites filled the ranks. But the name China Gang had stuck.

The Chinese cannery workers were adept at hand-butchering, cleaning and trimming fish, but early in the century a machine was invented that eliminated the need for many of the workers. One of the remarkable new contraptions could do the work of 12 men; it cleaned and dressed 3600 fish per hour and was given the insulting name Iron Chink.

Balclutha set off with Captain Bremer in command; he was a red-haired German in his mid-forties, muscular and even tempered. His reputation as a shipmaster was impeccable. A towboat moved the great windjammer through Bay waters. She passed in the wake of busy ferries and moved past the Presidio, where a band concert sent faint sounds wafting out to sea. At the Golden Gate a stiff breeze struck up, and the men scurried down for sweaters and coats. Dead ahead lay the vast gray Pacific, flecked with whitecaps. *Balclutha* was towed until the Farallon Islands thrust into view. Then she was set free, and the process of setting sail began, the loosening, the shaking out, the setting of the enormous rectangles of canvas. This was the job of the fishermen, who doubled as sailors during the voyage.

During the flurry of activity topside, the China Gang was settling down in the hold to a favorite pastime: gambling. On one side, a companionway was the official gaming table. A rambunctious crowd of Mexicans, Filipinos and Portuguese huddled round, some crouching, others standing; everyone was hooting. A candle at each end of the table lit their faces against the darkness of the hold. To the far side, a quieter scene was unfolding. Chinese in traditional pigtails sat on overturned buckets around a low trunk playing chuck-luck by lantern light.

One Chinese gambler survived very little of the journey. After several days at sea he succumbed to the ghastly conditions. "When the Chinese died aboard," Sommer explained, "we couldn't put them overboard. You had to deliver the body to the port of destination. That was a treaty. We had to deliver him to Karluk." Still two weeks from port, the crew applied a time-honored technique for stowing the body. "There was one man," Sommer continued, "who used to get $25 for putting them in those big salt beef barrels we saved. He put them in there and pickled them. Pickled them in brine and then sealed it up. It went ashore at Karluk and the Chinese would take care of it from then on."

When a fisherman died, later in the voyage, he was given an informal burial at sea. "We wrapped him up in canvas," Sommers said, "put some lead in there or pig iron and a piece of board over him and shoved him overboard. No particular ceremony."

Fishermen and China Gang workers were given separate treatment throughout the voyage, and since the China Gang was excluded from the sailors' union their conditions were dismal. A San Francisco newspaper reporter named Max Stern

Chinese cannery hands play fan tan on the forecastle head of the wooden bark Harvester *in 1899. The tug in the distance is towing the vessel out of Cook's Inlet in Alaska for the journey back to San Francisco. Chinese workers, called China Gangs, were regular features aboard ships, like* Harvester *and* Balclutha, *engaged in the Alaska salmon trade.*

posed as a regular member of a China Gang in 1922; his firsthand account sheds light on what conditions aboard *Balclutha* must have been like. Writing in the *San Francisco Daily News,* Stern reported:

> With our dirty little galley next to the toilet, our water pail under the steps, our rusty tin serving dishes and our two meals a day, lacking a table to eat from, serving ourselves and washing our own dishes in salt water, sans butter, fruit, dessert, succulent vegetables, milk of any variety, we made a sorry picture beside the fishermen.
>
> Often I would stand by the shiprail and watch steaming dishes go aft for the fishermen. Milk was always on their table and so was butter in plenty. Every day they had fruit and every dinner they had some dessert. Vegetables and several kinds of meat were not uncommon.
>
> Their coffee smelled like real coffee. Our mixture had three properties of coffee as I knew it. It was brown and it was warm and it was sweet. It tasted like no coffee I had ever met. Evidently brewed from some charred cereal, it had been treated with a touch of canned milk and sugar. I could hardly swallow it but it was our only beverage for the whole season.
>
> For breakfast we had mush, unsalted, little sugar, and over it was poured a chaulky [sic] solution called "southwest"—diluted condensed milk, watered until only the color of milk remained. For breakfast twice a week they had ham and eggs. Hot cakes and mush and milk, steak and all manner of other good things

warmed them on the cold journey. Instead of two meals, they had three, but that was not all; they had a second breakfast at 10 o'clock of coffee and cake and at three o'clock in the afternoon the bell rang again for coffee.

Seaman Sommer remembers eating well aboard *Balclutha.* "You had to do a lot of work," he said, "but they was feeding us wonderfully."

Food was not the only measure of inferior treatment given China Gang members. Reporter Stern could hardly bear the China Gang living quarters:

> There were 72 men in this China Gang, and all were packed into the little fo'castle. The air was heavy and stale to a sickening point. The place was hot with animal heat. I could hardly breathe. There was the stench of booze—and added to that was a new odor I had never encountered. It was, I later learned, the smoke of marahuana weed, the desert flower of the hemp that gives to the Mexican his hours of pleasant forgetfulness. . . . Over to the left of the fo'castle, where the Orientals had all gathered, hung the strong foreign odors of Chinatown, a mixture of tea, fish, opium and many other elements but dominated by the overpowering smell of Chinese tobacco. The fetid stink of sweating unwashed humans arose from every group and permeated the farthest corner of the "China Hole."

Stern noted a stark contrast in the fishermen's accommodations:

Down the middle of the fishermen's cabins was a table covered with oilcloth. Lamps swung aloft and a bucket of fresh water was always suspended near the end. The little rooms were crowded and the bunks were small and cramped but there was air aplenty and light in the daytime; a thing we would have given our souls for.

Balclutha sailed onward uneventfully until midnight of May 16. She raced through misty moonlight presumably on course within the 30-mile-wide strait between the Trinity Islands and Chirikof Island. Captain Bremer was on deck; he knew the strait and was expecting 30-fathom soundings. But something was amiss. He gave the order to shorten sail.

Seaman Sommer was high aloft on the main royal yard taking in that sail, but before he could execute the command the lookout cried out in alarm: land straight ahead. "When he called out," Sommer remembers, "we saw it right there. You could see the land and the snow. And right then and there she hit." The ship quivered and heeled. Still on high, Sommer clung to the yard as a deathly hush pervaded the night. After a moment, silence broke, pandemonium swept over the deck. Sommer jumped to a backstay and rode it down. "The rubber boots I had on just dropped off me. Just burned them off, sliding down there." He was greeted by wild-eyed fishermen racing up from below. The deck, now crowded with some 50 men, was angled at nearly 45 degrees; footing was unsure. There was talk of the ship capsizing.

From the forward 'tween decks came the soul-piercing wails of the China Gang. At the first sign of trouble the watchman had locked the companionway trapping the China Gang below, which appears to have been standard practice. Reporter Stern came across similar tales associated with the 1908 wreck of the *Star of Bengal* off southwest Alaska. "The sailors, so the legend goes, battened down the scuttle of the Chinese Hole to save themselves," he wrote. "It was their intent that the Chinese crew would perish while they got the boats. But it helped them not at all, for most of them drowned too." The *Star of Bengal* disaster was the worst in Alaska packing history, claiming 111 lives. Ninety-six of 106 China Gang members went down with 15 out of 32 fishermen. The master and first mate survived.

Aboard *Balclutha* the fishermen were fast becoming drunk. It is a tradition of shipwrecks that you guzzle whatever booze you can't carry with you. This may cause come clumsiness in releasing the lifeboats but at least the terror of the moment subsides. The animals were first to go overboard in order to clear the deck. "It was a simple matter to get the cattle overboard," Sommer reported. "We just shoved them, helped them along, opened the pens, out they go."

It was a mile swim to land, which happened to be one of the Geese Islands just off the southern end of Kodiak. Captain Bremer had strayed 50 miles northeast of his course and had entered the almost unnavigable Sitkinak Strait.

The livestock in any case proved a hardy breed. "The cattle got ashore alive," Sommer continued, adding that the sheep also made their way safely. "But the pigs were all dead. They couldn't make it. They clawed themselves to death."

The fishermen then abandoned ship, dropping their dories and heading for the beach. The remaining seamen turned their attention to the hysterical China Gang. "They were banging away down there," Sommer recalled. Several rescuers went to the bolted companionway. "They let out so many at a time. If anybody tried to rush out, the watchman had a belaying pin right there. He'd knock them right down. It was the only thing you could do. They were panicky, and I don't blame them. They were locked up in there like rats." Eventually the China Gang was herded into boats and guided toward land.

In the morning, the crew began ferrying supplies ashore from the crippled vessel, which was perched on a reef and heeled over with sails flapping. The next several days were spent ferrying supplies ashore. Camp was established with the fishermen and China Gang segregated in tents made of spare sails from *Balclutha's* sail locker.

Sommer remembers this as a time of feasting. "We just ate canned goods but they were good. There were lamb tongues, beef tongue and all kinds of delicacies. I never ate better at any time in the best restaurants as I ate in the shipwreck of the Balclutha when we were first on the beach." Captain Bremer interrupted the banquet to ask for a volunteer to sail the 75 miles to Karluk with news of the stranding. Sommer jumped forward; having studied navigation he was selected. A day of sailing alone in a fishing boat delivered him to cannery superintendent Menkovsky, who dispatched a small steamer to rescue the crew and supplies; *Balclutha* was one of his main supply ships for the season.

The rescue of the crew dragged on for more than a week; and it was so thorough even the pickled Chinese managed to make it to Karluk, where the Chinese on the island arranged a proper burial in their cemetery.

On shore, friction began to develop between Menkovsky and the sailors. The superintendent was disheartened at the prospect of an unpromising season and he wanted the sailors to stay to help recover the loss. The sailors demanded to be returned to their port of origin, a right accorded to shipwrecked American seamen. Menkovsky retaliated by withholding food and money, forcing the sailors to steal from some most unlikely victims. The men had picked up on a Chinese custom that brought mourners to the cemetery every few days laden with offerings of food and tobacco for the dead. "One of the things any seafaring man likes to have," Sommer confessed, "is tobacco. So we used to go out there and help ourselves from the Chinese graves."

The wreck of the *Balclutha* was not the disaster it might have been; although a major incident, it was just one in the string of incidents highlighting her long career. Fortunately no lives were lost; in fact, there was more panic than actual danger, thanks to calm seas on the fateful night. The one great casualty was the ship itself. In his report of May 25, Captain Bremer described her as a total wreck. But the Alaska Packers Association had another idea and sent a representative to inspect the vessel. In 1904 *Balclutha* was 18 years old and, in operating condition, worth $50,000. The Alaska Packers' agent, looking to add to the company's huge fleet, offered $500, which Bremer, acting on behalf of owners Pope and Talbot, accepted. After

Star of Alaska *setting sail off the Golden Gate in the early 1920s. The fore and main (lower sails on the first two masts) have not yet been set.*

52

an arduous salvage job that dragged into July 1905, *Balclutha* returned to San Francisco for a complete refitting.

In the spring of 1906 she set sail again as she had in 1904 for the Alaskan salmon waters. This time she had a new name, *Star of Alaska,* and a new owner, whom she would serve admirably for 24 years. Her new skipper was Nick Wagner, who later reported that on the day of the great San Francisco earthquake *Star of Alaska* made a fast 63 miles in four hours. Wagner's daughter, Joan Lowell, wrote a best-seller about sailing with her father in the late 1920s called *Cradle of the Deep*.

In 1929, *Star of Alaska* made her final voyage north under sail, the last of an antiquated breed of square-rigged sailing ships tirelessly chasing the silver horde. Then, after 19 years as a gaudy show-boat, she became the first restored historic ship of the Maritime Museum Association.

3. The Sailing Schooner C. A. Thayer

*I*T DIDN'T TAKE LONG FOR WORD to spread back in 1848. And what a precious word it was, buzzing from lip to lip: gold, gold, gold, gold, gold. It spread to the villages and towns of California, leapt borders to Mexico and Central and South America. It was swept to New York, Boston and Philadelphia. Wherever it went it always ricocheted home, bringing back hordes of eager fortune seekers.

The gold rush thrust the sleepy Bay village of San Francisco into the headlines. Her name recently changed from Yerba Buena, the town had only 850 people and some 200 buildings and an encampment of tents, sheds and outhouses.

But by the summer of 1848, 2000 prospectors had swarmed through on their way to the banks of the American River in the Sacramento Valley. Two years later, 40,000 to 50,000 men had expanded the diggin's to include the Yuba and Feather rivers and the Sierra Nevada. San Francisco's population swelled to 25,000, and every night newcomers had to scramble for beds. Some wound up huddling under canvas shelters or building their own wretched shanties. Others put up at boarding

At first the State of California was puzzled by what to do with C. A. Thayer arriving from Puget Sound. Officials berthed her temporarily at a spare berth at Angel Island in 1958.

In the coastal lumber trade, two-masted schooners preceded the type of vessel C. A. Thayer represents. Here, seven "one topmast" schooners are gathered at loading chutes at West Port on the Mendocino coast.

houses if they could afford it. The price of a cot or bunk might run as high as $15 a night; for a few bucks less you could stretch out on a tabletop.

The scarcity of housing was indeed a problem (some knocked-down houses had even been brought from New England in the holds of sailing ships), but a long-term solution was soon in coming. Miners trudging north of San Francisco along the Sonoma-Mendocino coast brought back tales of vast redwood forests so dense the sun failed to penetrate. From Bodega Head to Humboldt Bay, some 400 miles, there seemed an inexhaustible supply of the colossal trees, averaging 300 feet in height and 20 feet in diameter. So gigantic were they that 20 five-room houses could be built with lumber from just one tree; and the wood was resistant to fire and slow to decay, making it an excellent choice as well for use as railroad ties, then much in demand as the great transcontinental railway crept toward completion.

Most lumber reaching California in the 1840s came from the Sandwich Islands; in view of the abundant resources in California's own backyard, this now seemed impractical. Business logic demanded the exploitation of the nearby forests, but one question still stumped the lumbermen: how do you get millions of board feet of lumber from the forests to the towns? The answer spawned an entire shipbuilding industry.

The first sailing lumber schooners (of which *C. A. Thayer* is a late model) began hauling redwood timber along the coast in the 1850s. The development of the schooner followed the spread of lumber mills into the forest. Among the first lumbermen was Harry Meiggs, the notorious San Francisco alderman and grafter. In 1852, on bluffs overlooking the ocean, he established the California Lumber Company in a settlement that became Mendocino City. By 1860, 300 small sawmills had invaded the redwoods. By 1885, the Humboldt forests alone had 400.

Getting the lumber from the forests to California markets was a new and dangerous adventure. There were no wharves along the rugged redwood coast — nothing you could fairly call a port. Schooners usually had to tack through fog and inshore swells into shallow coves or "dogholes," though the relief these offered from wind and wave was slight. Some schooners were as small as 65 feet,

A classic view of an apron chute awaiting the arrival of a schooner. The chutes, which guided sawed lumber and railroad ties to the schooners' decks, were found along the Sonoma and Mendocino coasts.

57

but the men aboard were seasoned sailors, veterans of the deep-sea trade lured to coastwise service by the promise of good food, good pay and frequent stays in port. They expected danger. Coastal waters were so tricky, the dogholes so treacherous, that a slight mishandling of the vessel could prove disastrous. And danger did not disappear once a safe landing had been effected; it was then time to begin

*Two "one topmast"
schooners, also called
"outside porters,"
load simultaneously
under apron chutes at
outside port of
Bourns Landing on
the Sonoma coast.
Small cars on rails (at
right) bring lumber to
the chutes.*

the bone-wearying task of loading timber. Since the mills operated high on bluffs typically some 75 feet above the water, wooden slides or chutes had been built to send the lumber hurtling down to the ships' decks.

Capt. Carl Rydell, a veteran of coastwise traffic, had a few scrapes with death during loading operations:

The lumber is sent down the chute, near the end of which a man operates a brake to check the lumber as it leaves the chute. As each man gets a piece of timber he runs with it, lays it down exactly where it belongs, and returns to the chute. When the hold is full, the deck is loaded, the larger part of the cargo of a lumber schooner going on deck. The work goes well enough when the water is comparatively smooth; but when the vessel rolls, the chute during some moments is high above the deck. This makes it difficult for a man below to catch a timber at the right instant and get the right hold. If he makes a single slip, or if the man at the brake does not apply it in time, he may be injured or killed.

The small two-masters (known to sailors as "one topmost schooners" or "outside porters") were the first of the lumber vessels and flourished from the 1850s to the 1880s; they were so abundant that a sailor counted over 50 outbound vessels of this type becalmed one day in the lee of Point Reyes. As the lumber industry expanded, the small schooners gave way to three-masters and then to four- and a few five-masters.

C. A. Thayer, built by Hans Bendixsen at Fairhaven, California, in 1895, is large for a three-master (156 feet long, 36 feet beam). She carried about three times as much lumber (575,000 board feet) as the two-masted ships. Owned and operated by the E. K. Wood Lumber Company with a mill at Hoquiam, Washington, she was not immune to the perils of coastwise sailing. She had two serious mishaps during voyages from the company's mill to southern ports. The first, in November 1903, landed her ashore on the north spit of Grays Harbor; she was later floated off with only the loss of a rudder. In 1912 she set off from Hoquiam for San Francisco and ran into severe weather just off Eureka. The sea was so turbulent that her seams opened. After several tense hours the crew escaped safely, but *C. A. Thayer* was in need of extensive repair and re-caulking and had to be towed to San Francisco.

Thayer's damage alone might have been enough to force her from the lumber trade. But there was another factor that led the E. K. Wood Lumber Company to sell the vessel. By 1912, steam power was speeding up business along the redwood coast. In a few years, steam schooners were to nudge sailing ships from the coastal trade altogether. One great advantage of steam power was that it made getting into and out of the troublesome dogholes and bar ports much safer. Sailing schooners were entirely at the mercy of the elements; with steam power, control lay more firmly in the hands of the shipmaster.

The early steam engines, simple compounds installed in existing sailing schooners, put about 100 horsepower into a single propeller for a top speed of eight knots. These coal-burning conversions of the 1880s were few in number and eventually gave way to much larger, specially built steam vessels equipped with triple-expansion oil-burning engines; by 1911, fewer than a dozen coal-burning steam schooners still operated on the West Coast.

From their modest beginnings (the early steam schooner *Newsboy* measured only 218 tons), the new ships came to dominate the lumber trade. Eventually, single-ended steam schooners of con-

siderable size, such as the 951-ton *Wapama*, were built. Now a prized possession of the National Park Service, *Wapama* was on display at the Hyde Street Pier from 1963 to 1979, when she was removed for refurbishing. Despite mounting costs and repeated delays, it is hoped that this last of some 225 wooden steam schooners will soon return to her place on the waterfront.

Wapama is typical of the ships that muscled sailing schooners like *C. A. Thayer* out of the lumber industry. She was built in 1915 by the St. Helens Shipbuilding Company of St. Helens, Oregon, but she is in part a Bay Area product. Her wooden hull of Douglas fir was built near the forests of the Northwest, but her engine was manufactured and installed in San Francisco. Her cargo capacity, 1.05 million board feet of lumber, measures nearly twice that of *C. A. Thayer.* A "single-ended" steam schooner (engine room and superstructure aft), she also has compact quarters for 45 fare-paying passengers. There is a spacious lounge on the upper deck and a dining saloon below, the two linked by a curving staircase.

A favorite scheme of unscrupulous ticket agents was to place travelers aboard ships like *Wapama* after promising elegant voyages on great ocean liners. Capt. Hugo Clever, then a *Wapama* sailor in San Pedro, remembers being ordered to meet the train bringing *Wapama*'s passengers for the trip north. He and his mates had unloaded lumber, then loaded cement, before setting off to the depot. "We looked like a bunch of—well, the worst you could ever see. Just cement on us from one end to the other." They greeted their charges merrily and escorted them toward the steam schooner, baggage in hand. The conversation, according to Clever, went something like this:

C. A. Thayer, *owned by the State of California, was photographed in 1957 in the straits of Juan de Fuca as she departed for her new home and new role as a museum ship.*

61

"Where you going with my baggage?" a traveler asked.

"On the ship."

"That's not the ship."

"Sure that's the ship. That's the *Wapama.*"

"Sometimes they wouldn't let us have the baggage," Clever recalled. "Those poor fellows what bought tickets for the *Wapama.*"

Whatever the complaints of the passengers, their hardship could never equal that of the crew. As one sailor put it: "Great grub, fine pay, but work to kill you." For 12 hours a day, the men took turns hauling the loads of lumber by hand in and out of the hold and on and off the deck (on deck using hand-held "molle" hooks). So it went; sometimes for three days almost nonstop. The work was etched in the sailors' hands. Crew member Emmett Hoskins remembered: "When you turned into your bunk at night, your fingers were all curled. For a while your hand was shaped like holding a hook. Your hand gets so tough you are not bothered by blisters or anything like that. My hands got so tough they were almost immune to cold weather."

When the men weren't breaking their backs hauling lumber, they were gathered round the card table playing poker. Dogtired, their bones bent from labor, they nonetheless gambled intensely for long hours. The ship's cook sold beer and whisky, and entire paychecks were won or lost in an evening. One cardsharp summed it up: "Well, you see, you have nothing to worry about. You're all by yourself and you have as good a time as you can. You work hard, drink hard, and play hard."

Wapama's rough and tumble lumbering days eventually came to a close; during the depression she was sold to the White Flyer Line to provide general cargo and passenger service between San Pedro and San Francisco. She was then sold to the Alaskan Transportation Company prior to World War II and kept steaming until 1947, when she wound up in the hands of a scrap dealer in Seattle. The Maritime Museum, using funds supplied by the state of California, rescued her in 1956, preserving not only a vintage vessel but the last wooden steam schooner from a fleet of 225 built on the West Coast.

Although steam schooners like *Wapama* edged sailing schooners out of the lumber trade, many windjammers continued to thrive in other services. When *C. A. Thayer* stopped hauling lumber in 1912, she took up a second career in the salt-salmon industry. For the next 12 years she made annual voyages to Bristol Bay, each fall bringing the salmon pack from the saltery of "Whitehead Pete" Nelson, a prominent figure in the trade, to San Francisco. Then in 1925 she began her third career, this time in the cod-fishing industry under the ownership of Capt. J. E. Shields of Poulsbo, Washington. When she was finally retired in 1950, *C. A. Thayer* was the last sailing ship in commercial use on the Pacific Coast.

According to a fisherman named Jimmy Crooks, life aboard the codfish schooners was severe. In 1926 Crooks signed aboard *Fanny Dutard,* a schooner similar to *C. A. Thayer,* and his account is a tale of little pay, constant danger and considerable pain. It throws light on what conditions must have been like aboard many schooners in the cod-fishing industry.

Crooks' first eye-opener was the rather unsporting system of payment. If for any reason no fish were delivered at season's end (because of foul weather, shipwreck or other mishap), no fisherman was paid. Wages were based on the catch, and even in favorable years pay was shockingly low: 1-1/2 cents per pound. "It soon became obvious," Crooks complained, "that I would have to catch one hell of a lot of fish to even make wages corresponding to the lowest paid laborer on shore."

On the voyage north, he was quartered with the other fishermen below the main deck. It was a dungeon with no portholes, dimly lit by cheap kerosene lamps. A breath of air fluttered through a small scuttle but brought little relief to the unwashed herd occupying cramped bunks. Bedbugs, fleas and lice shared the quarters, and the stench of rotten fish and stinking bilge water nauseated nearly everyone.

Yet, throughout the trip to the fishing grounds, the hardy souls pounded away day and night, preparing their equipment for the upcoming season. A huge potbellied stove and anvil were positioned between the rows of bunks. Lead was cut, melted and molded into sinkers. Reels for hand lines were carved from wood. Spreaders and swivels, gaff-hooks and even small windlasses, masts and booms for their dories were fashioned in the primitive workshop. Crooks kept one eye on his work and

In 1912, C. A. Thayer was sold for a new trade. Owned by a well-known Scandinavian, "Whitehead Pete" Nelson, she became a salmon packet running to Alaska. Here, Nelson's wife, Hilda, sits on the wheelbox. Of sailing north, she had this to say: "Vell, in the Thayer, ve had to go this vay, and that vay, and this vay, and that vay . . . and sometimes, ve couldn't go at all . . . They call it, 'Heave to' . . ."

Harlan Trott, a Christian Science Monitor *reporter, made the voyage aboard* C. A. Thayer *and recounted his experience in a book,* The Schooner That Came Home. *Here, Trott is seen in the codfish forecastle.*

another on his mates, who, in the main, had come aboard straight from prison. Local bootleggers had a nefarious system whereby they sprung sailors serving time for nonpayment of booze debts on the expectation that when the men returned from the sea they'd have enough money to pay off outstanding debts and to plunge headlong into the new year's binge. The sailors were, in essence, captive to a vicious cycle.

After nearly three weeks at sea, an edgy Jimmy Crooks finally escaped the cramped, foul-smelling fishermens' hold. It was time to begin work. Anchored at 45 fathoms, the men launched their little dories into the freezing Bering Sea. Exhilarated at finally leaving the ship, the fishermen drifted off in solitary pursuit, one man per dory.

Crooks remembered:

> Once he cast off his dory from the schooner, each fisherman was entirely on his own. He was master of all he surveyed, and it would take all his skill and judgment to survive the months ahead of him. When the time came to fight for survival in the southeast gales that spring up in the Bering Sea almost without warning, there would be nobody to consult or seek advice from, and all that would count would be skill in seamanship and confidence in his ability to keep calm and be free from fear.

Crooks may have reproached his fellow seamen for their slovenly habits and their weakness for

After C. A. Thayer *made the last commercial voyage by a sailing ship under the American flag in 1950, she was sold to an entrepreneur who displayed her as a pirate ship on Hoods Canal, Washington.*

65

drink, but he had the highest praise for their performance at sea. His mates were "the most skillful seamen" he had ever associated with and "the hardest workers and most fearless men" he had ever seen. "A person had to be tough to survive alone for even one season," he concluded, "but to return

Jack Dickerhoff, the last of San Francisco's master riggers from the sailing ship days, was chief mate on C. A. Thayer's voyage down the coast.

The boats slipped easily into the powerful currents and drifted far from the mother ship, becoming flecks on the horizon.

The men fished with two hand lines, one on each side of the dory. One line always remained in the water while the other was provided with fresh bait; this was because cod tend to lose interest if not constantly tempted. Each line carried a heavy lead sinker and two hooks. On a good run, a fisherman could return with about 320 fish, the dory's capacity.

Any fish under eight inches in length was unacceptable by the terms of the fisherman's contract. While this diminished the catch, it also attracted the seaman's faithful companion: the hungry seagull. Each flap of the bird's wing stirred aeons of marine folklore; the stories have it that the seagull is in fact a shipwrecked sailor resurrected from a watery grave. And the bird's easy compatibility with ships and sailors did much to perpetuate the myth. Jimmy Crooks seemed mystified. "By some means," he pondered, "the gulls seem to know when we caught a small fish on our lines, and they would arrive at our dory just in time to grab the fish when we threw it back into the ocean." The fisherman and the seagull often struck up a friendship. "Some gulls became very tame and adopted individual dories," Crooks wrote. "And it was not unusual to have one hitching a ride on the end of the boom, or when cutting fish for bait to have one reach out and help himself to tidbits which he fancied."

year after year to this particular occupation he had to be absolutely immune to hardship and danger."

The hardship began early every morning. After a four o'clock breakfast, the men battled their blistered hands and hauled at the brine-stiffened halyards to launch the dories. In minutes, a flotilla was fanning out in a semicircle astern of the schooner.

In the early part of the season the men took full advantage of the 24-hour daylight, making two or three trips from the mother ship per day and working to utter exhaustion. Often unable to sleep in their infested bunks, they sometimes lost precious time snoozing in their dories; some dropped anchor to catch a few winks, others drifted aimlessly with the tide.

The men put a premium on protecting their health, especially since there was no medicine chest and no qualified medical help aboard the schooner. Several contracted fish poisoning and recovered at sea. Jimmy Crooks was not so lucky. One day he was aloft on the boom when he lost his footing and fell into a barrel. He might have escaped with just a bad case of embarrassment but the barrel contained several sharp fishing knives, one of which sliced through his finger. In a few days the wound was festering, and regular soaking in Epsom salts and water offered little relief. The poor seaman could find no peace. He paced the deck day and night as the fish poison crept up his arm to his neck. The ship's master was reluctant to interrupt the good fishing, but he relented when Crooks became delirious. At the last moment, he put the injured man ashore.

"What I will never forget," Crooks wrote, "is standing before the doctor at the cannery with a hand like a ball of pus and wrapped in an old piece of shirt, and the fact that the doctor would not give me any medical attention until the owner of the vessel could be contacted and he was sure he would be paid for his service." Despite Jimmy Crooks' condition, he managed to survive and provide us with his vivid account of cod fishing in the Bering Sea.

C. A. Thayer was a codfisher from 1925 to 1931; then declining prices for salt cod laid her up for 10 years. During World War II she was conscripted as an Army barge and used to store empty shells from target practice at sea. After the war Captain Shields restored her masts, using those from his four-masted schooner the *Sophie Christenson,* and she became a codfisher again, making five voyages between 1946 and 1950. By this time, consumers were losing their taste for salted cod, and although *C. A. Thayer* was still an efficient vessel, she was retired until the Maritime Museum persuaded the state of California to buy her in 1957 for permanent preservation.

4. The Scow Schooner *Alma*

*T*HE SIGHT OF *ALMA* the little scow schooner on San Francisco Bay hardly inspired poetic reverie. She's squat and boxlike, and when she passed in the shadow of majestic square-riggers she was usually weighted down with bales of hay stacked high on her deck. She had no high-sea adventures tucked within her Douglas fir planking; no, she never even ventured beyond inland channels. *Alma* is one of about 400 local scow schooners, an anonymous hardworking breed that once hauled hay, bricks and chicken feed along waterways from San Jose to Sacramento.

Why, then, did three ship preservationists brave a long night on the Alviso mudflats 25 years ago to save the little scow from extinction?

It was August 17, 1959. The tide had been rising steadily, but by midnight it still wasn't high enough. The charts promised that this was the night; in fact, this was very likely to be the last chance to salvage her. The Alviso tidelands, where *Alma* had been beached two years before, were fast becoming landfill; the scow was already nearly landlocked by seashells and rubble, and the next predicted high tide was two months off.

Alma departs the bay wharves at the mouth of Mission Creek, San Francisco, with a partial cargo of hay. The tarpaulins over the hay bales indicate that rain is expected. The Key Route Pier at Oakland appears over the yawl boat she is towing.

Three men—Maritime Museum curator Karl Kortum, historian Roger Olmsted and ship conservator Harry Dring—were prepared to stay the night, if necessary, to float her free. The alternative was unthinkable. This little scow was a living monument to a 100-year tradition of San Francisco maritime commerce. She may have lacked conventional beauty, but she had carried the goods that helped build the entire Bay Area. An estimated 400 scow schooners had been built on San Francisco Bay, and *Alma* was the last still in existence. Hers was a vital chapter in local history.

When her plight had become known, curator Kortum had jumped into action with a call to Sacramento. (At this time, San Francisco's historic ships were under the California State Parks Department.) Deputy Director of the Department of Natural Resources Edward Dolder rushed through authorization to purchase the scow for $500, and soon all that stood in the way was the slowly rising tide.

Finally, at one in the morning, the moment arrived. Mooring lines were run from *Alma* to a power boat; the engines revved, and the scow was drawn gently into the channel, where she rested for the night. The next day she was escorted to an Oakland shipyard by a tug operator who turned out to be a grandson of the scow's first owner, James Peterson. It was an auspicious beginning for the old scow's new life.

San Francisco scows date back to the gold rush, when shipping on the Bay and its tributaries yielded enormous profits—so great, in fact, that vessels of every shape and size battled for a cut. But the rivers, sloughs and creeks did not favor standard sloops and schooners. Sharp bows and round bottoms were obstacles in shallow-water loading and unloading operations.

The solution was magnificently simple: build vessels specially suited to the conditions of San Francisco Bay waterways. Of course, scows had been in use in other parts of the country before 1850, but the ones built in San Francisco were of a distinctly local variation. The aim was maximum utility at the lowest cost. Great seaworthiness—useful in the ocean—was sacrificed for a simple hull design. The standard model had a shallow draft for navigating shallow waterways, a flat bottom for stability while loading on mud, and square bow and stern for easy maneuvering in narrow inlets. Its heavy centerboard structure included a drop keel to make the craft weatherly. The carrying capacity was twice the scow's tonnage.

Alma's design is somewhat unusual. Instead of standard planking running lengthwise on her flat bottom, hers runs from side to side for greater strength. Her size is average: 59 feet long by 22.6 feet wide.

Like many of her sisters, *Alma* was constructed

Two vessels now in the National Park Service fleet, photographed together in the first decade of this century. Balclutha is at the same berth she occupies today and Alma (center) has brought a cargo of grain to be loaded aboard the steamer at right.

in the shipwright's own yard. Fred Siemer, a German immigrant, built her in 1891 for his son-in-law, James Peterson, and named her after Peterson's daughter, Alma. Mrs. Alma Peterson Sooman, now 97 years old, recalled the early days in an interview several years ago. Her account details another era, a slower, pastoral time in San Francisco, the era of the scow. She grew up on Hudson Street in Hunters Point, then the center of scow-building operations. "We had to walk from Hunters Point to the streetcar on Third, eight blocks over muddy hills. We'd run into flocks of sheep, and pigs and cattle. And they'd have men on horseback, taking care of them. That's all a thing of the past now, no more."

The way scows were built is also only a memory. Alma Peterson was just three years old when *Alma* first sailed, but the scow's construction made an impact on her. "There was a little dirt road in front of the house and then the beach. They kind of dug out some of the dirt to make the ways. And it was built right in front of our house."

Her father, James Peterson, owned and managed six scows in a field where most haulers operated independently with a single boat. A Swedish immigrant, Peterson was a quiet man who educated himself with a Bible and a dictionary. He spent most of his life at sea and, typical of many scow men, escaped from deepwater sailing to the comparative comforts and short voyages of the inland water-

ways. His scow-schooner business eventually grew into one of San Francisco's largest.

Much in the construction of *Alma* was left to the inclination and prejudices of Siemer, the shipwright. This was standard practice. Building plans were virtually unheard of, the lack giving each scow its own individual quality.

When it came time to restore *Alma,* however, the lack of a plan presented some tough challenges, especially since she underwent several structural changes during her long career. An intriguing bit of detective work went into discovering the height and size of her original masts. First it was necessary to determine the diameter of the spar, based on her existing mast hole; then, by applying a formula, it was possible to recreate accurate measurements. Pieces of other scows had to act as stand-ins during the restoration. But, through use of old photos, a few plans drawn from scows still existing in the 1930s and other evidence, such as the mast hole, *Alma* eventually became both a picture of her old self and a composite of all scow types.

Whatever the design variations, most scows were two-mast gaff schooners; a few smaller ones were sloop rigged. Usually they also carried a jib and gaff topsail to catch wind blowing over treetops along the banks of channels and they sometimes set a main topmast stay-sail called a fisherman.

A two- or three-man crew (usually two men and

Alma *brings lumber to the headwaters of Petaluma Creek, discharging near the Washington Street bridge, circa 1911–1912. Lumber and grain were common upriver cargoes for scow schooners. Hay was a typical load on the trip back to San Francisco.*

73

a boy) guided the scows along hundreds of miles of navigable waters to such tiny "ports" of the South Bay as Alviso, Newark and Ravenswood; the scows roamed the shallow "creeks" to Petaluma, Napa and Sonoma as well as the deeper reaches found in the Sacramento and San Joaquin rivers. The season generally lasted from spring to fall, when prevailing westerlies blew from astern when going upstream. These breezes often pushed even well-laden scows at eight to ten knots. But their travels were not always without mishap. *Alma,* herself, took a starring role in one minor incident in 1909. She collided with the Alaska Packers steel steamer *Kvichak* and came out the clear loser. A published report of the accident said it was nothing serious—*Alma* turned turtle, lost 500 bags of fertilizer and was righted by the tug. In fact, she lost $5500 worth of cargo as well as the citizenship papers of her master and sustained $2000 worth of damage. *Kvichak* steamed off unscathed.

Just as the wind sometimes blew a scow into another vessel (though quite infrequently), it was also known to drop entirely on occasion in the fall and winter, leaving the craft becalmed. At these times, the crew used a method called jayhawking. With the help of the windlass, usually the only machinery aboard, the men moved the scow forward by running a line to a tree on the bank and hauling up to it. Other means of making progress included poling, kedging (laying out an anchor and heaving in on the line) and even rowing. In spells of calm the less ambitious crews were to be seen lounging on deck fishing or duck shooting; sometimes the men would steal into nearby orchards and help themselves to the best of the season's finest crop.

Sailing brought its share of headaches, but in the scowman's daily routine it proved far less demanding than loading and unloading cargo. Fierce battles broke out as scows jockeyed for position along the wharves; crews resorted to any means necessary to beat back the competition for coveted dock space. It's no wonder, then, that scow owners chose their deckhands from the toughest sailors.

Once cargoes were safely ashore or loaded on board, the scows wasted no time turning round and heading out on the next tide. It was a gruelling cycle, not interrupted by fatigue or poor weather. Alma Peterson Sooman recalls that rain seldom stopped her father and brothers from sailing; they simply covered the load with a huge tarpaulin.

By far the most important load in the scows' early days was hay. The frequent sight of the little boats lumbering along precariously overladen earned them the nickname hay scows. What oil is to the 20th century, hay was to the 19th; a hundred years ago the world moved on hay. And at one time scows had nearly the entire local hay trade to them-

Fred Siemer (far right) leans on a horse capstan bar in his shipyard at Hunter's Point. The capstan has just been used to haul out Alma (left) for the annual overhaul of her hull.

75

selves. Bales were piled so high on deck that the helmsman's steering wheel had to be raised on a special platform so he could find his way to the bustling hay market at the mouth of the Third Street Channel. One old-timer bristled at the suggestion that he even needed such a platform. "See?" he growled, "I don't need to see. Hell, I could smell my way here."

The scow and her crew led a tough day-to-day life, but sometimes the grind gave way to pleasure. Owners chartered out their boats for Bay parties, known in some quarters as "drownding parties."

These were festive outings with music and dancing on the scow's broad deck and lots of booze. Invariably someone would fall overboard, usually with comic effect but also on rare occasions with tragic results.

The owners themselves threw a party in the spring to celebrate the beginning of the new hauling season. The scows, freshly scraped and painted, would set off toward popular Paradise Cove on the Tiburon peninsula for a day of picnicking and swimming. Alma Peterson Sooman has pleasant memories of those special days. "We had a big crowd. We'd take the husbands and the wives and the kids and old friends. We'd get over there and drink beer. Spend the day." For drinkers who wanted a nip on the sail over, Alma's father had a wooden keg of beer permanently stowed in the scow's hold.

Seventy-five years later Alma Sooman could still feel the chill from the trip home in the evening. "We'd come back at night. It'd be so cold coming past the Golden Gate. The fog and the rough water and the dark! They know the bay, though. They always managed all right."

The last sailing scow had been built in 1906, and, with the development of the internal combustion engine, it soon became apparent that *Alma* would have to bow to progress in order to remain profitable. Wind power was giving way to motor propulsion so rapidly that by 1925 only four sailing scows could be found on Bay waters. *Alma* was one of the last to convert, finally taking an engine aboard in 1927.

The shift from sail to motor occurred swiftly because conversion was relatively easy. Mostly it involved cutting off the bowsprit, removing the mainmast and installing a pair of cheap engines. Early engines were very large and heavy but dependable and economical; they usually had 20 to 40 horsepower, though some had greater potential. *Alma*'s later engines, two oil screws installed in 1951, had a total of 220 horsepower.

With these modern advances, the scow's cargo changed, too. Petaluma was emerging as the egg basket of the world in the 1920s, and many scows, *Alma* among them, began transporting calcium-rich oyster shells from San Francisco Bay's east and south shoals to the farms of the North Bay. Chickens must have calcium in their diets to produce eggs with hard shells.

Nothing, however, could have sustained the scow as a profitable vessel. Even with engines installed, the number of working scows declined precipitously in the 1930s, and by 1940 few were following the old familiar routes. Water shipping in general was suffering because of vast improvements in roads, construction of trans-bay bridges, and a proliferation of trucks that were able to provide what waterbound scows could not: door-to-door service.

Nevertheless, *Alma* battled against her fate operating as a shell dredger until 1957, when she was the last scow schooner at work on San Francisco Bay. It was two years later when the three ship preservationists waited through the night to float her free on the high tide, saving a valuable relic of San Francisco's early days of shipping.

5. The Ferryboat *Eureka*

*E*UREKA IS AS LONG AS A FOOT-BALL FIELD; she has as many windows as a five-story office building. In her heyday, her vast decks packed in 2300 passengers. But on February 10, 1957 she edged away from the Oakland mole looking a bit hollow with only 121 passengers aboard.

It was the late-night, 11:40 P.M. departure, but just how late it was for *Eureka* didn't become clear until she churned into the open Bay. Moments into the four-mile, 18-minute trip to San Francisco something dreadful happened. There was a snap and a mild jolt and the *Eureka* drifted, powerless; the main crankpin of her gigantic walking-beam engine had broken.

For 20 years she had steamed across the Bay in defiance of the bridges, refusing to follow her sister ships to the scrapyard. But this was to be the last night for the stubborn paddlewheeler; her huge walking beam and cylinder had separated. She was forced to succumb. Tugs towed the crippled vessel back to Oakland; and her passengers, loaded onto

The newly created Eureka, formerly Ukiah, departs from her slip at the Ferry Building in San Francisco. From 1929 to 1938, she was sometimes loaned on a Sunday night to the Golden Gate ferry system to relieve passenger load and operated from Hyde Street Pier where she is currently berthed.

Eureka receives her newly constructed walking beam engine at Moore Drydock, Oakland, next door to the Southern Pacific shipyard, July 24, 1926.

buses, rode over the water to the Ferry Building by the only means available: the San Francisco – Oakland Bay Bridge.

In better days, the typical ferry crossing was a moment when ordinary landlubbers escaped from the routine; had their hair ruffled by a sea breeze; shivered in the chilled mist of the open Bay. And there were the views, the glimpses that caused jaws

to drop, the sights so full of mood and color. George Harlan (1967), longtime chronicler of ferryboat lore, wrote of "the exultation I always experienced when, returning from a trip, I would stand on the forward upper deck of the ferryboat and see the city rising out of the Bay, gilded with the gold of the setting sun, or silvered with the phantom fog. Today I know that much of my love of San Francisco was born of those upper-deck views of the city."

Passengers first admired San Francisco from the decks of a Bay ferryboat in 1850. For the gold-rush-inflated price of $1 (or $4 if you brought a wagon or horse), you could cross between the city and San Antonio Creek, now the Oakland Estuary, aboard the screw-propeller steamer *Kangaroo*. According to the publicity, she offered San Franciscans an "opportunity to visit the wondrously wooded region of Contra Costa." The trip proved quite popular, and from the twice-weekly service of a single vessel, the ferry business blossomed. Captains of small ocean-going sidewheelers who had steamed around the Horn from the eastern seaboard saw profit and a good life in the ferryboat business. Many stayed in San Francisco, leaping vigorously into the competition. After all, who wouldn't prefer the tides and fog of the Bay over the wild and unpredictable waters of the open sea?

Independent ferry companies took to the water and operated successfully for a few years. Then the railroad men moved in and bought out the small operators. The railway companies regarded the Bay as an extension of their tracks; by adding ferries to their lines they were able to provide uninterrupted travel throughout the Bay Area, linking water and rail. By the 1860s, such pioneers in the ferry business as Charles Minturn, who started the Contra Costa Steam Navigation Company in 1852, were selling their boats to the railroad companies.

One of the largest early railroads to operate ferries was the Central Pacific, incorporated in 1861 by four Sacramento merchants who later were known as the Big Four: Leland Stanford, Collis P. Huntington, Charles Crocker and Mark Hopkins. As the Central Pacific absorbed ferry companies and smaller rail lines it outgrew the established terminal facilities at Davis Street. A search for a new location culminated in the building of San Francisco's first ferry building at the foot of Market Street. The new station on East Street, now the Embarcadero, welcomed its first ferry passengers on September 4, 1875.

One ship that docked regularly at the ferry building was a steamer that had begun life with a different name and design. *Chrysopolis,* an old river steamer built in 1860, was bought by the Central Pacific Railroad Company in 1874. The railroad set about transforming her into an efficient Bay ferry, and when she emerged from the shipyard for regular service a year later she had become the *Oakland,* a double-ended ferryboat 261 feet in length. Double-ended design improved travel speed by eliminating the need for turning around in the Bay.

Massive rebuilding was not unique to the *Oakland. Eureka* was built in 1890 as the railway-car-and-passenger ferry *Ukiah*; her principal function was moving railroad cars from the railhead at Tiburon to San Francisco. In 1920 she lost her name and received a whole new superstructure, being transformed into a passenger-auto ferry. She was two years in the Southern Pacific shipyard on Oakland Estuary before she was ready to serve as the *Eureka* on the Sausalito — San Francisco run.

Capt. A. R. Gustofson, who piloted both *Eureka* and *Ukiah,* remembered the new *Eureka* as a smooth-handling ship. "As big as she was," he said, "she was about the fastest ferryboat there was on San Francisco Bay. She made the trip from the San Francisco ferry building to Sausalito under favorable conditions in 27 minutes, 6-1/2 miles. She was a fast boat."

For most of her career, *Eureka* operated from the current Ferry Building at the foot of Market Street. This structure replaced the earlier Central Pacific Terminal in 1903 in order to keep pace with the ever-expanding ferry business. Passengers entered the building under an imposing clock tower modeled after a cathedral belltower in Seville,

In 1922, Ukiah was stripped of her superstructure in the Southern Pacific shipyard on the Oakland Estuary and rebuilt from a car float into a full-passenger ferry, the largest in the world. The dismantling affords a rare view of a walking beam engine in its four-story majesty. Note the diamond-shaped walking beam at the top of the structure.

Spain, and boarded from upper and lower landings that corresponded with the ferryboat's decks. This two-level process speeded the loading and unloading of passengers.

Once everyone was aboard, watch officers in blue serge uniforms with gold trim quickly prepared the ship for departure. The second officer raised the gangplanks, and deckhands cast off the bow lines. The second officer then flashed a hand signal to the first officer in the pilot house, who pulled a bell cord; this notified the captain of the ship's readiness. The captain sounded the whistle and signalled the engine room to open her up to "full speed ahead." Ever so slowly, the paddle wheels began rotating, building up speed until the boat finally eased out into the Bay. The crew was so skilled in the procedures that casting off (and tying up) took no more than a minute or two.

Once under way the captain and crew relied on expert seamanship for a safe passage; they were aided by no mechanical navigation equipment. No radar, no loran, no radio direction finder, no gyroscopic compass, no fathometer—only a standard compass, which was rarely consulted. The captain's sharpest instruments were his eyes and ears.

In foggy weather, ferryboats made their way cautiously by sound alone. The captain handed the wheel over to the first officer and concentrated on the bells and whistles of nearby ships, making sure all the while that his own whistle sounded at regular intervals. A lookout helped guide the captain by pointing in the direction of nearby whistle blasts.

Eureka *passes* Santa Clara *on San Francisco Bay.*

With one hand on the steering lever and the other on the engine room telegraph, the captain cons Eureka *into a safe landing at her slip at the Ferry Building.*

Although an occasional collision or close call did occur, the crossings were remarkably safe. In peak years, nearly 50 ferries traveled Bay routes simultaneously, and statistics show that loss of life was one-millionth of a percent.

Despite the odds against it, death did strike on November 30, 1901 in one of the most notable of ferryboat incidents. The events of this night in-spired Jack London to write his story *The Sea-Wolf.*

The steamer *San Rafael,* piloted by Captain John Taylor MacKenzie, churned slowly out into a fog-shrouded Bay at 6:10 in the evening commute. To the tune of slow, rhythmic whistle blasts she made her way toward Sausalito, unaware that the large paddlewheeler *Sausalito* heading toward San Francisco was on a direct collision course. Just off Alca-traz Island, the *Sausalito* rammed the *San Rafael,* knocking a gaping hole in the smaller ship's side just aft of the paddlebox. At first most passengers were unalarmed, a deck hand circulated advising everyone to slip on a life jacket merely as a pre-caution. As the passengers waited calmly the crew lashed the vessels together and secured a plank for escape onto the *Sausalito.* In a short time, nearly everyone had crossed safely to the undamaged ves-sel and the *San Rafael* was set free. Despite the lack of alarm, the severity of the collision killed three people. The other great loss was the *San Rafael* herself; once speedy and graceful, she slipped for-ever from the surface of Bay waters. Going down with her was Old Dick, a horse kept aboard for hauling express carts on and off at terminals. The animal refused to cross the gangplank to safety, pre-ferring instead to remain on deck, where he was as much a crew member as the men in the blue serge uniforms. Eventually, the captain of the *Sausalito,* John Tribble, was held responsible for the collision; he was discharged.

Though not nearly as eventful as the *San Rafael*'s final excursion, the day-to-day commute did have a certain cyclical excitement. In the morning, groggy passengers kept an eye on their watches and another on their coffee cups; in the evening the weary throng steamed happily away from the headaches of the workplace. Author Richard Reinhardt (1978), once a ferryboat commuter himself, captured the disparate moods elegantly: "The morning trip was brisk, a purposive throb of engines, a nip of salt air, a rush to the coffee shop . . . the homeward trip was softer, quieter: bronze sky, pink water and a trailing plume of gulls above the wake."

Hovering seagulls were a common sight, and a good bit of lore grew up around them. Peg-leg Pete, for one, was a longtime friend of the commuter. Thousands of passengers on one crossing or another saw him hanging above the stern, dropping and rising with the breeze, his fierce body and muscular wings keeping him close. He was a healthy bird in every respect except his one-leggedness. (The other probably was lost in avian battle.) But Peg-leg was not unique. His was the name attached to several gulls, all matching the Peg-leg Pete description.

Aside from birdwatching, passengers might wander into the restaurant for a brisk meal, play cards, or loiter at the newsstand or snackbar. For the best food, you had to ride on the Key Route

In her heyday, crowd scenes like this were common on Eureka's *foredeck and stairs (left).*

85

System. Office workers were known to pass the afternoon hours at their desks longing for the Key Route corned beef hash and apple pie, followed of course by the Key Route coffee, a special blend found nowhere else.

For the most part, commuter recreation on the homeward journey set a leisurely pace. "In the main saloon," Richard Reinhardt remembered (1978), "shoppers from Fruitvale would slip off

Eureka's hull. The ferry is sheathed with sheets of copper in the same traditional way as the old Cape Horn square-riggers. This was to prevent ship-worms (teredo nava-lis) from destroying her wooden hull.

86

their shoes and dig into the latest *Delineator* to catch up on the world of Jean Harlow and Norma Shearer. On the upper deck, captains of industry would share the joys of Culbertson contract bridge, Acme Beer and vicarious adventures in the *National Geographic*."

Ferry travel brought out a certain forgetfulness in some passengers, who would leave behind everything from umbrellas to children. H. Ellison, superintendent of the Southern Pacific ferries in 1921, tells in the *San Francisco Daily News* of the time a baby was absentmindedly abandoned and rode alone twice across the Bay before the frantic mother realized her mistake.

On another occasion, a deckhand spotted an odd cabinet on a bench. When he opened it to check for the owner's name, scores of insects and butterflies rushed to the top. The deckhand also found a two-pound box of chocolates inside. An hour later, an elderly naturalist appeared at the superintendent's office to claim the cabinet and its unusual contents, explaining that he'd gathered the specimens in the Contra Costa County hills.

By far the most common item left behind was the vanity bag. "Funny thing," Ellison says, "you'd think these women carried something valuable in their little vanity cases. Usually they just contained a powder puff, a lipstick, and two hairpins. Sometimes a crumpled dirty handkerchief, and sometimes a few cents in change." Single gloves also turned up regularly. But, Ellison claims, never a pair.

A forgotten child, a boxful of bugs; these were minor inconveniences to the ferryboat crew. Some passengers, however, excited serious alarm. In the days before the Golden Gate Bridge, the distraught turned to the ferryboats to put a romantic end to their lives. But a leap from the upper deck of the largest ferry offered only a short drop, and even the most troubled souls rarely aimed for a landing forward of the paddles, where they were certain to be crushed in the huge rotating wheels.

A. R. Gustofson, once captain of the *Eureka*, remembered lowering the rescue boat on several occasions. "We saved them all," he said, "except one who must've been weighted down. He never came up."

A favorite pastime of those aboard was peering into the vast engine room, which occupied nearly the entire hold area. On the early ferryboats, passengers were able to view the workings of the massive beam engines through glass panes. From the lower deck they saw a maze of cams and levers, dials and bells. Amid the clanging bells and revolving camshaft the engineer performed a dockside departing ritual, pulling down on the starting bar to open the valve ports at one moment, raising the bar the next moment and up and down until the vac-

THE LAST 5:15

uum pump, crank, and paddle wheels all churned in rhythm.

From the upper deck, passengers watched the main cylinder rod, usually no less than 60 inches in diameter, pump 20 to 24 times a minute.

Eureka's walking-beam engine extends some four stories high; its main cylinder is 65 inches in diameter. Each 12-foot-long stroke of the piston drove the great walking beam up and down to turn a 27-foot-wide paddlewheel.

The huge walking-beam engine is perhaps the best remembered feature of the ferryboats. It was the engine that pioneered steamboating on inland waterways, an engine for which no better substitute for driving paddle wheels was ever found.

In times of emergency, walking beams came to the rescue. During San Francisco's greatest disaster, the April 1906 earthquake and fire, ferryboats carried the helpless free of charge from the ravaged city to friends and relatives in Oakland and Marin. Southern Pacific opened its warehouse facilities to the homeless; the fire-fighting equipment, medical supplies, food and clothing all came by rail, then ferryboat.

In happier times there were festive rail-ferry excursions to Felton and Big Trees in the Santa Cruz Mountains. Clubs and organizations chartered boats for pleasure cruises. One group, The California Camera Club, used to steam around the Bay capturing the ferryboat era on film.

And well that they might. For it gradually became apparent that the day of paddlewheelers was not to last forever. Ferryboat transportation reached its peak in 1930 when 6 million vehicles and more than 40 million people traveled across the Bay. But with the completion of the San Francisco – Oakland Bay Bridge in 1936 and the Golden Gate Bridge in 1937, commuters took to the road.

Soon ferry company boats were placed on laid-up status, sold for scrap or demoted to service as fish reduction plants. Two ships, the *Piedmont* and the *Oakland,* were resurrected from mothballs to provide ferry service to the 1939 World's Fair on Treasure Island. It was a short-lived revival, they ended their careers for good with the close of the fair in 1940.

Eureka made her last departure from Oakland in 1957. With just two boats remaining, Southern Pacific ferries managed to keep Oakland service alive for another year. Finally, the *San Leandro* was the only ferryboat remaining and she tied up for the last time on July 30, 1958, ending 100 years of stately ferryboat crossings on San Francisco Bay.

A new breed of excursion-boat ferry service between San Francisco and Marin County began in 1971, a result of the planning and promotion of Harlan Soeten, former curator of the Maritime Museum. The sleek modern vessels offer the same exhilarating wind-swept crossing; but to discover the splendor of a paddle-wheel adventure, you must stroll across the broad wooden decks of the *Eureka,* elegantly restored and on display at the Hyde Street Pier.

6. The Liberty Ship Jeremiah O'Brien

*I*T'S A WONDER ANYONE was excited by the old liberty ship. When Capt. Thomas J. Patterson first spotted her in 1962, she wasn't much of a sight. Her masts were stumpy, her funnel squat, her steel plates streaked with Cosmoline preservative, her bottom covered with barnacles. But to Patterson, what a beauty!

His orders in 1962 were to scrap some 300 liberty ships in the United States reserve fleets along the West Coast. But his inspection turned up an unusual one: the *Jeremiah O'Brien,* unusual because after 19 years she still bore the stamp of her first day of service. Beneath the barnacles and peeling paint was a historical treasure. "*O'Brien* is in excellent shape," Patterson announced, "as if she had just returned from World War II."

The ship was like a time capsule. Inside were all the original furniture, doors and linoleum table-tops. Wartime maps plotting her last missions were tacked up in the chart room. Yellowing messages hung on bulkheads. The radio room, complete with 1943 equipment, looked as though the operator had stepped out for a smoke.

Every other ship in the Suisun Bay reserve fleet

As the National Liberty Ship Memorial, Jeremiah O'Brien *is berthed at Pier 3 east, Fort Mason Center.*

Streaked with rust and grime from thirty-six years in mothballs, Jeremiah O'Brien *is towed to a new life as the National Liberty Ship Memorial.*

had undergone some form of modification. Bulkheads had been knocked out, plating changed, gear tacked on or taken away. But the *Jeremiah O'Brien* was untouched. She was the last unaltered liberty ship.

Patterson was ecstatic, but his orders were to scrap the vessels, *O'Brien* included. To buy some time, he placed *O'Brien* at the bottom of the list and set about devising a plan to save her.

O'Brien and her sister ships had poured out of emergency shipyards during World War II much the way Henry Ford used to hustle Model A's along the assembly line: one after the other, no stopping, no variation. It was a shipbuilding program born of desperation. In the early days of the conflict, the German war machine was trampling British defenses and nowhere was the devastation more evident than at sea. In the first nine months, German U-boats had sunk 150 British ships, severely disrupting ocean supply lines.

In February 1941, President Franklin Roosevelt went on nationwide radio to announce an emergency shipbuilding plan to aid the British. At the time, German subs and surface raiders were sinking more than 500,000 tons of Allied shipping each month in the North Atlantic alone. Heralding the President's plan, one newspaper proclaimed: "Sea Scows with Blunt Bows Will Carry the Tools to Britain."

But before the first keel was laid, liberty ships had an image problem. In his broadcast, Roosevelt had referred to them as dreadful looking objects. He was a fancier of floating beauties, and liberties, emergency cargo steamers that they were, sacrificed visual appeal for practicality and speed of production. Rear Adm. Emory S. Land, who presented the blueprints to the President, reported that "He came to the profile sheet, backed away from it and said, 'Admiral, I think this ship will do us very well. She'll carry a good load. She isn't much to look at, though, is she? A real ugly duckling.'"

An ugly duckling. The press liked the term, spread it across front pages nationwide, and liberties have worn it through history. In an effort to bolster the ship's image, Admiral Land proclaimed the day of the first launching, September 27, 1941, as Liberty Fleet Day. Speaking before a crowd of thousands at Bethlehem-Fairfield shipyard in Baltimore, he promised that this liberty fleet was just the beginning. "As long as America faces the crisis and challenge of Hitlerism," the admiral boomed, "there will be a continuous and increasing flow of ships from this and other American plants." The Baltimore Civic Band struck up a rousing rendition of the "Star-Spangled Banner" and the first ship, the *Patrick Henry,* moved down the ways. What was first designated an ugly duckling slid into the water exalted as a liberty ship.

Following the first liberty were 2750 more over the next four years. Their contribution to the war effort cannot be overestimated. Leonard Sawyer writes in his book *The Liberty Ships* (1970) that the vessel "is accredited with saving not only Britain, not only the Allied cause, but the whole world from disaster—for there was a grave fear that the war might be lost simply because Allied lifelines were stretched beyond the limit owing to an insufficient number of ships."

The broad shipbuilding program including liberties, tankers and cargo vessels did not gear up full scale until after the bombing of Pearl Harbor in December 1941. President Roosevelt ordered a sevenfold expansion, requiring 2300 vessels totaling 23 million deadweight tons to be built in 1942 and 1943. About 1500 were to be liberties. The country responded with such enthusiasm that in early 1942 Rear Adm. Howard Vickery, vice-chairman of the United States Maritime Commission,

Jeremiah O'Brien *slides down the ways at her launching in June 1943 at the New England Shipbuilding Corporation in South Portland, Maine.*

94

could write, in *Marine Engineering and Shipping Review*: "Our nation is now in a position to build more ships than all other countries combined—friend or foe."

This was indeed an enterprise of unprecedented scope. Forty-eight shipyards in 21 states achieved an average of one ship launching and three keel layings a day. By the fall of 1942, Vickery could expect three launchings a day. Of course, the shipyards did not work alone. More than 500 manufacturing plants in 32 states were supplying them with ship parts: boilers, rudder fittings and cargo booms from Tennessee, lifeboats from Indiana, bulkheads and hull steel from Kentucky and West Virginia, hawser reels from Illinois. It was a grand project on a typically grand American scale, each plant and person holding to the ideal, working to the peak of ability, making deliveries on time. Construction speed records were established, then broken. The Kaiser Shipyard in Richmond, California, turned out its first liberty in 197 days. In August 1942 the Kaiser yard in Portland, Oregon, delivered the *Pierre S. DuPont* in 31 days. Then the Richmond yard completed the *Joseph W. Teal* in 16 days.

One phenomenal Kaiser record will stand for all time. In a burst of patriotic zeal a gang of flangers, welders and shipfitters raced the clock to assemble an entire liberty in just 4 days, 15 hours. More than 250,000 parts, including a 130-ton engine, went into

place between November 8 and November 12, 1942, when the *Robert E. Peary* stood poised for launching.

Liberties bore the Maritime Commission designation EC2. (E stands for emergency, C for cargo, 2 for large capacity.) They were designed on the model of an old, reliable British tramp freighter of 1879. After the war, some controversy arose over the origin of the design; the ship's exceptional performance inspired a variety of people to seek credit. Admiral Land, however, laid the question to rest in the December 1960 *U.S. Naval Institute Proceedings:* "Various claims for the Liberty ship design have been made by U.S. citizens," he wrote, "even a gold medal was awarded for one, but they were erroneous and no award was deserved. The Liberty was based on an old tramp ship design." He went on to name the naval architects—Gibbs and Cox of New York—and to elaborate on the influence of the British model.

The design was adapted to meet the requirements of war: low cost, rapid construction and simple operation. To save time and steel, welding was preferred and prefabrication of major structural parts speeded up assembly. Concessions and compromises had to be struck to keep progress at a steady rate. A prime example is the Maritime Commission's plan for obtaining a vast number of engines with little delay. The engines, it was decided, would have to be less advanced than originally desired. An older type of triple-expansion reciprocating steam engine was used because idle plants around the country could gear up for its immediate production.

The engine powered the standard-sized liberty: length 441 feet, 6 inches; beam 57 feet. Her loaded draft was 28 feet, total displacement 14,000 tons, and gross tonnage about 7500. With a full load of fuel she carried 9146 tons of cargo, which might include either 2840 jeeps, 440 light tanks, 230 million pounds of rifle ammunition or 3,440,000 C-rations. The simple design permitted emergency repairs in virtually any port in the world.

Once in the water, the vessel moved more like a swan than an ugly duckling, at least according to Maritime Commission vice-chairman Vickery. Writing in *Marine Engineering and Shipping Review,* Vickery said, "The Liberty Ship presents a trim, seagoing appearance. Riding low in the water, with its long, slender prow and its simple straight-lined superstructure, it will knife its way through the waves as gracefully as any vessel afloat."

Assembling ships was a filthy, noisy task. Just what worker conditions in the shipyard were like is preserved in a book by Joseph Fabry called *Swing Shift* (1982). Written in 1943 and tucked into a desk drawer until 1980, Fabry's account blends the cold steel of liberty-ship construction with the personal trials of the gang on Assembly Way Five at Kaiser's Richmond Shipyard No. 2.

Fabry's first day in the yard was an eye-opener. But he quickly eased into "the great adventure of helping to build ships for victory" with a bunch of guys who "looked as though they had dug coal with their bare hands and wiped their hands on their faces."

After passing through the shipyard gate under a sign reading REMEMBER PEARL HARBOR, he saw:

> A procession of tin hats, overalls and lunch boxes, crowding into a new world—piles of steel plates of all shapes and sizes, shacks and booths, ladders and scaffolds, posters like the one reminding you that the guy who relaxes is helping the Axis. The yard was arranged city-like: F, G, H streets, running in one direction, 9th, 10th, 11th streets in another. It was a city without houses, but the traffic was heavy. Cranes, trucks, trains noised by. Finally, after a rather long walk, I came to the edge of the water. There were the ships—or rather, halves, thirds, quarters and tenths of ships. There was a piece of ship here and a piece of ship there, and a hole in between. And then out of a clear sky a crane dropped the missing piece of ship, big as a house, into that hole.

Shipyards had sprung up in such rapid succession that the labor force of qualified workers was soon exhausted. Thousands of men and women who had never seen a ship before poured into the yard to build liberties. Shipyard schools were established to train welders, shipfitters, electricians and joiners. By 1943 the number of shipyard workers reached 700,000, as compared to less than 100,000 during the busiest peacetime years.

Even the men at the top were new to shipbuilding. Henry J. Kaiser, one-time owner of a New York photographic shop, started out in construction with sand and gravel interests and moved on to such herculean projects as Hoover Dam and the San Francisco Bay Bridge. He came to shipbuilding as a genius of mass production and garnered newspaper accolades, such as: "Henry Kaiser, who knew nothing of shipbuilding two years ago, has just completed a ship in 47 days." Kaiser regarded his ships as assembly-line products; he spoke of their "front" and "back" ends. Because he was free of preconceived notions about traditional shipbuilding, notions that might have slowed down another man, he was able to turn his energetic naiveté to great advantage. He simply saw what was needed and set about accomplishing it with the greatest efficiency.

Salesmen, farmers, students—people from all walks, people who might never have been brought together—all swelled the ranks of shipyard workers. "All you needed were two hands," Fabry writes (1982), "and if you had only one, they'd find a job for your one hand." Women, too, signed up in great numbers. At one time, they made up more than 30 percent of the work force at the shipyards. Rosie the Riveter became a popular national image, winding up as a Norman Rockwell cover of the *Saturday Evening Post*. Women contributed to all spheres of construction, but most worked as welders, earning themselves another nickname: Wendy the Welder.

When Fabry's gang learned that women would soon work side by side with them, the men became confused. "Steel and skirts," Fabry wrote, "the idea is too big. Steel and skirts—the thing isn't right. Powder puffs and iron. It won't work."

But it did. Women's presence enlivened many work crews, romances flowered and competition between the sexes brought out the best efforts in both. One woman in Fabry's gang was awarded a $50 bond for her inventiveness. After one of her male coworkers was injured, she was inspired to create a new safety device, for which she earned the first prize given to a woman by the Labor Management Committee.

Over 100 liberties were named after women, both the famous and the little known. There were the *Amelia Earhart*, the *Betsy Ross*, the *Dolley Madison*, the *Pocahontas* and the *Emma Lazarus*. Emma Lazarus? She wrote the freedom call inscribed on the Statue of Liberty:

Give me your tired; your poor

Your huddled masses yearning to breathe
    free
The wretched refuse of your teeming
    shore
Send these, the homeless, tempest-tossed
    to me:
I lift my lamp beside the golden door.

Naming 2751 ships was an assembly-line head-ache in itself. Only the names of outstanding Americans no longer alive were to grace the bows of liberties, according to Maritime Commission guidelines. As the number of ships grew the names became more and more obscure, to the point where the Maritime Commission was launching the *Hans Heg* and the *Hawkins Fudske*. Besides 493 senators and congressmen, 157 cabinet members, 248 state and territorial governors, 208 regional heroes and pioneers, there were 14 musicians and 7 philosophers. Eventually the guidelines were relaxed.

Named and freshly painted wartime gray, a liberty ship still did not take aboard a single bag of grain or round of ammunition until it passed a series of rigid seaworthiness tests. The Maritime Commission's trial board went for a two-day outing with throttles opened wide. A full crew demonstrated the ship's readiness by spinning her wheel on a dizzying course, swinging her in circles, running her astern full speed. All the while trial board members combed the ship from forepeak to poop, listening to her purr, testing her fuel consumption, her horsepower, surveying her holds, inspecting her equipment, pipes, wiring, and safety devices.

Despite the exhaustive testing, liberty ships did on occasion fail at sea. In December, 1943 two liberties split apart and sank, followed in early 1944 by the *John Straub* breaking in two; it sank in the Arctic. Critics of welding, still a fairly new process, created such a stir that the Secretary of the Navy ordered an investigation of welded construction. After studying more than 2000 liberties, investigators determined that structural failure caused loss of life in only one case: that of the *John P. Gaines,* which broke up 40 miles south of Chirikof Island in frigid Alaskan waters. Eleven men were lost. Estimates were that 12-1/2 percent of all liberties had welding defects. Sometimes they slipped by during testing; in most cases there were no serious consequences.

The liberty set sail with a complement of 44 officers and crew, all members of the civilian merchant marine. These were not fighting men of the armed forces but peacetime sailors ordinarily engaged in international commerce who now had come face to face with war.

Wartime demands for shipping put a strain on the merchant marine force, pushing it from 65,000 men in 1940 to 250,000 by 1945. To accommodate such expansion, the merchant marine admitted

In May 1980, a restored Jeremiah O'Brien *left Bethlehem shipyard and went for a Seaman's Memorial Cruise before docking at her home berth, Pier 3 east, Fort Mason Center.*

boys too young and men too old for the draft. Many liberty crewmen had never seen a ship before, much less sailed one.

In November 1941, Congress acknowledged that American merchant ships, now steaming into dan- gerous waters, warranted protection; it authorized the positioning aboard of naval armed guards. Equipped with what has been described as a pea- shooter armament, the ships took on a 15- to 20- man crew to operate a 3-inch, .50-caliber gun at the

A crane lowers a 3-inch 50 caliber gun onto the deck of Jeremiah O'Brien adding to the ship's wartime authenticity.

bow, a 5-inch, .38-caliber at the stern and eight 20-mm guns for antiaircraft defense. The additional men did not cramp the merchant marine crew unduly, although some doubling up was necessary. Friction sometimes surfaced between the two groups, however, because Navy gunners resented the merchant mariners' higher pay; the disparity seemed unjustified since all men shared the same ship and the same dangers.

Quarters did grow quite cramped when the ships became transport vessels carrying an additional load of several hundred troops to the front. The voyages seemed interminable. Hal Rubin, writing in *Oceans Magazine,* remembers being one of 500 servicemen sharing the hold of a liberty en route to Europe. Locked below deck for the month-long trip, many men became seasick. The day-to-day business of life was far from routine.

Feeding several hundred men from a galley designed for forty, meant that the passengers—those who were well enough to spend several hours daily in a chow line—subsisted mainly on sandwiches and stew. Water for bathing was rationed and a quick, once-a-week shower was a luxury. In bad weather the troops were restricted to their bunks or to a few open spots in the overcrowded hold. On infrequent calm days we were allowed on deck in small groups for exercise and a breath of fresh air. During one smooth spell we staged some boxing matches with a wooden hatch cover as the ring. Otherwise, the tedium was lifted only by floating crap and card games. The available pocket books were worn out long before we reached port.

In less crowded conditions, sailing aboard a liberty offered considerable comfort. The officers' and crew's quarters were all in one house, eliminating the need for men to pass over weather decks to reach messes. Officers were able to retreat to private rooms; crewmen slept two or three to a room. Officers and crew ate at separate sittings, the officers in the "saloon," the crew in another dining area. And one luxury for all were the showers, a great leap forward from the merchant seaman's traditional bucket-washings.

Usually the Navy armed guards' quarters were divided between the main deck and the after deckhouse, the roughest spot during a storm. To pass the long hours, the armed guards were issued an entertainment kit containing a punching bag, boxing gloves, medicine ball and a variety of games: chess, checkers, cribbage and dominoes.

Judging from complaints filed with the National Maritime Union, the merchant seaman's lot appears to have been quite tolerable. One crew requested an electric ice-cream mixer, another wanted a pop-up toaster for the engine room; a third put in for better-tasting breakfast cereal. Among the more serious requests was a call for helmets and gas masks for every man aboard.

These were hardly unreasonable or extravagant demands, especially in light of the missions undertaken by these men. Liberties travelled wherever troops or supplies were needed, the most notorious run being the one to Murmansk, Russia. At least 800 ships risked bombing, strafing and torpedoing on this run, and storms and drifting ice could slow progress to two or three knots. Moving in convoys and protected by United States destroyers, 97 ships on the Murmansk route still did not reach their destinations.

In the Mediterranean, liberties encountered a new danger: Italian frogmen who attached mines to the hulls of ships at dock. Air attacks in this region were also a constant threat, since the ships operated near enemy air bases. In April 1944 German bombers streaked low over a convoy near Algiers, focused on the *Paul Hamilton,* which was brimming with explosives, and struck right on target. The ship was blown out of the water and the lives of 504 men went up in black smoke; it was the war's worst human disaster involving a liberty ship.

In the Pacific, liberties added another hazard to their growing list: fanatical kamikaze attacks. During the invasion of Okinawa, liberties braved a shower of conventional bombs and the diving assaults of at least 2000 kamikazes to deliver some of the 182,821 troops, 746,850 tons of supplies and 503,555 tons of vehicles needed for battle. When the sand had settled, the ships reversed course and ferried the victorious troops safely home again. In his book *Liberty Ships—The Ugly Ducklings of World War II* (1972), John Gorley Bunker reports that Gen. Douglas MacArthur had only the highest praise for the accomplishments of the merchant marines: "When it was humanly possible," MacArthur said, "when their ships were not blown out from under them by bombs or torpedoes, they have delivered their cargoes to us who need them so badly. In war it is performance that counts."

During the winter and spring of 1944, prior to the massive landing at Normandy, liberties fed supplies to troops in Southern England awaiting word to move. And when the armada edged into the channel, liberties sailed too, carrying ammunition, guns, food and equipment needed for the invasion. After the landing, liberties joined the shuttle between England and France, keeping a stream of reinforcements flowing. The *Jeremiah O'Brien* made 11 supply shuttles, at one point carrying part of General Patton's Fifth Division from Belfast, Ireland, to the Normandy coast. Author John Bunker (1972) records the scene one liberty captain described: "The channel is the busiest thoroughfare in the world. Craft of every description are traversing it day and night and often there doesn't seem to be enough room to squeeze another ship through."

The crew of the *Jeremiah O'Brien* had known the massive operation was planned, but they were kept guessing about its date. In May, they sailed for Scotland and trained in the use of gas masks; this was a precaution against the possible dispersion of poison gas by the Germans. From Scotland the *O'Brien* sailed for Southampton, staying close to the English coast the entire way. In June, troops and equipment were loaded aboard, and the assault began.

The war at an end, liberties were to be found in a variety of peacetime roles. Many entered worldwide commercial shipping; usually, the only alteration needed was the stripping of armaments, gun tubs and surplus life rafts. Some, cut in half and stretched another 60 to 80 feet, were converted into bulk carriers and container ships. The Italians even added Fiat direct-drive engines to make motorships out of liberties. The *Jeremiah O'Brien* was retired from service on February 7, 1946 and sat in the national reserve fleet at Suisun Bay for more than 33 years waiting to be reactivated.

The United States Navy retained some liberties for conversion to radar picket ships, technical research ships and other specialized duties. Over the years, their value in most spheres waned, and the government turned to scrapping to eliminate the old workhorses. In 1960 a large-scale scrapping program began, the program that led Captain Thomas Patterson to stand before the *Jeremiah O'Brien*.

Saving the *Jeremiah O'Brien* required the help

of hundreds of volunteers and thousands of dollars in donations. The first step was the establishment of the National Liberty Ship Memorial in 1978, a non-profit corporation to direct the project. The memorial pooled the expertise of steamship company heads, union leaders, shipyard bosses, government representatives and eager ship lovers. An early success was the enrollment of the *Jeremiah O'Brien* in the National Register of Historic Places. Then came a $10,000 grant from the National Trust for Historic Preservation to restore the ship's aging woodwork. The maritime industry delved generously into its coffers, to the tune of $600,000 in services and materials, and the Department of the Interior, the National Trust for Historic Preservation and the state of California added nearly $450,000.

But the money would have been nothing without the ceaseless devotion of many people. Harry Dring, then conservator of San Francisco's historic ships, credits the participation of workers from machinist, electrician and shipyard unions; these men along with scores of others labored through the summer of 1979 to revive the *Jeremiah O'Brien's* triple-expansion reciprocating steam engine. On October 4, after weeks of cleaning preservatives from the boilers, the volunteers chose an engineer, oiler and fireman and a decisive test began. Most of the men down in the engine room on this day had stood watches in similar engine rooms nearly 35 years before. As the oil-fired furnaces were lighted

Chief Engineer Harry Morgan (right) watches as Fireman Bob Webnau tends the oil-fired furnaces in the liberty ship's engine room.

103

and the pressure climbed, they were transported back in time by the familiar sounds of the pumps and the smell of escaping steam. The engineer waited for the pressure to reach 240 pounds, then opened the throttle; the pistons began moving smoothly and, to a circle of smiles, the engine turned over. It was a success charged with nostalgia for chief engineer Harry Morgan and his all-volunteer crew.

Two days later, *Jeremiah O'Brien* set sail under her own steam from Suisun Bay to the Bethlehem Steel Corporation shipyard in San Francisco, where *O'Brien* was scraped of barnacles and weeds, sandblasted and given a fresh coat of paint—World War II gray.

On May 21, 1980 the old liberty left the Bethlehem yard for a Seaman's Memorial Cruise around the bay, sailing under the Golden Gate Bridge before docking at her home berth—Pier 3 east, Fort Mason Center, in the Golden Gate National Recreation Area. For a vessel built to last only five years, the ship has shown a spirit of defiance characteristic of her namesake, the original Jeremiah O'Brien.

Who was this man? His story comes from a different war, the American war of independence, and the rebellious townfolk of Machias, Maine. These people, hearing of the battles at Lexington and Concord, decided to show some resistance of their own. In May 1775 they stripped a pine tree of its foliage, leaving growth only at the top, and mounted it on high ground. This, they said, was their liberty pole, and gathering round they vowed to defy the British at all costs.

When two 80-ton British sloops, the *Unity* and the *Polly,* pulled into port in June, the townfolk had their chance. The ships were brimming with provisions, and it was customary for the people of Machias to trade lumber from the town mills for the goods aboard ship. But the village businessmen were not about to give up their lumber to aid the British occupation forces in Boston; they refused the exchange.

Capt. Ichabod Jones, owner of the *Unity* and the *Polly,* turned the matter over to Captain Moore and his 100-ton armed escort vessel, the *Margaretta.* Captain Moore first ordered the removal of the liberty pole. Perhaps, he may have reasoned, he could undercut the people's will by eliminating the symbol of their defiance; he never had the chance to know. Jeremiah O'Brien's younger brother, John, challenged the order, causing Captain Moore to issue an ultimatum. "That liberty pole must come down," he warned, "or it will be my painful duty to fire upon the town."

Far from intimidating anyone, Captain Moore had only spurred the townfolk into action. Shortly, a band of heavily armed Machias men in small boats and canoes was in hot pursuit of Captain Moore and the *Margaretta.* Despite his powerful armament, Captain Moore just fired a few warning shots over the village and set sail. At a safe distance downriver he issued a second warning: if Captain Jones or his ships were harmed, the *Margaretta* would return to burn the town. This threat prompted a second band of young men to leap aboard Captain Jones's ship the *Unity* and seize her, all without firing a shot. The townsfolk now had a ship large enough to engage the *Margaretta*.

Through his spyglass, Captain Moore watched as the captured *Unity* was loaded with 20 shotguns, a small cannon, 30 hay forks, a few axes and 35 feisty volunteers. The supplies did not look like peace offerings, so Captain Moore hoisted anchor and retreated farther downriver to Holmes' Bay.

The *Unity* gave chase with 30-year-old Jeremiah O'Brien in command. Among the crew were his five younger brothers. Keen sailing soon brought the *Unity* within striking distance of the *Margaretta,* which had had an hour's head start. Captain O'Brien ordered Moore to surrender; but the Britisher refused and opened fire with a stern swivel gun, killing two of O'Brien's crew. In return, a backwoods moosehunter aboard the *Unity* dropped the *Margaretta*'s helmsman with a ball through the head. O'Brien then maneuvered his ship alongside the other and lashed the two together in a volley of gunfire and hand grenades. A marksman aboard the *Unity* set his sights on the foul Captain Moore and connected with deadly precision, leaving the *Margaretta* leaderless. Still, it took an hour's battle, some of it hand to hand, to subdue the British crew. Captain Jeremiah O'Brien boarded the captured vessel and hauled down the British ensign himself. *Margaretta*'s weapons were transferred to the *Unity* and, with her new name the *Machias Liberty,* she became the first American armed cruiser of the Revolution.

O'Brien's antics did not sit well with the British. In July 1775 they sent the armed cruiser *Diligent* and her tender *Tapnaquish* "to bring the obstreperous Irish-Yankee in for trial." But O'Brien was not to be chastened; using the armed strength of the *Machias Liberty* he captured both vessels. His luck ran out, however, in 1776—the British finally captured him, shipping him off to England as a prisoner of war. Even then the indefatigable captain managed to escape. Just as the war was ending he made his way back across the Atlantic and, having played his part in freeing the colonies, O'Brien settled into the quiet life of Machias. He worked as a customs collector until his death at age 74. That O'Brien's been memorialized in the naming of a ship termed a liberty is a particularly apt remembrance of his deeds.

7. The World War II Submarine Pampanito

*F*HE BITTERSWEET RESCUE occurred in September 1944. In debris-strewn waters of the South China Sea, the submarine *Pampanito* spotted what appeared to be life rafts bobbing on the horizon. She closed in slowly, wary of a Japanese trap. In the distance, several dozen figures began to take shape clinging to rafts, timber, hatch covers — anything that floated.

From the sub, crewmen could make out that some of the figures were waving; others were stretched out limp and lifeless. As the sub came near, cries from the water reached the deck; the crew was astonished. Then the cries became more distinct, and the crewmen now crowded topside burst into hoots of elation. *Pampanito,* it seemed, had crossed paths with a scattering of shipwrecked Englishmen and Australians. A miraculous chance encounter! Or was it?

With heroic care the crew brought the survivors aboard. Many were too weak to speak, but those with voices began unfolding a shocking story of terror and deprivation in the jungles of Burma and Thailand. The men had been prisoners of war; they built the infamous "Railway of Death," an enemy

Tugs Trojan *and* Sea Fox *maneuver* Pampanito *in the Stockton Deep Water Channel turning basin in 1982.*

Healthy POWs plucked from the sea mingle with Pampanito *crewmen topside.*

108

railroad through 265 miles of dense jungle. They had slaved for more than a year, had been fed little and were subjected to harsh beatings. When the job was done they were herded onto Japanese passenger-cargo ships sailing for Nippon. In midcourse the ships encountered a wolf pack of three United States submarines and were blown from the water.

The jaws of the *Pampanito* crewmen fell open. *Pampanito,* the heroic rescue ship, had been one of the three attacking submarines.

Pampanito's adventure had begun when orders came during the night and early morning of September 9 and 10. The Fleet Radio Unit, Pacific (FRUPAC) stationed at Pearl Harbor had intercepted Japanese messages detailing the course of an important convoy of six ships and several escorts. The order from Commander Richard G. Voge, chief operations officer at FRUPAC: destroy those vessels, stop their cargoes of oil, rubber, tin, copra and scrap metal from feeding the Japanese war machine.

Pampanito was to rendezvous with two other subs in a wolf pack code-named Ben's Busters at 115 degrees east longitude, 18 degrees 40 minutes north latitude, the middle of the South China Sea. The pack's commander was Thomas Benjamin Oakley, Jr., skipper of the submarine *Growler*; *Pampanito*'s captain was Commander Paul E. Summers. and the third vessel, *Sealion,* had Commander Eli T. Reich in charge.

Pampanito was built at Portsmouth, New Hampshire, in 1943; she is a submarine of the Balao class, 312 feet long with a 27-foot beam, 12-1/2-foot draft and displacement of 1,500 tons. To take her down tanks positioned within the outer hull fill with water; to bring her up, compressed air is shot into the tanks to blow the water out.

Before the fateful rendezvous, *Pampanito* had had a checkered history of war service. She had been nearly depth-charged out of commission while on patrol in the Marianas. On another occasion, she narrowly escaped annihilation when two Japanese torpedoes hurtled past wide of the mark. Adding to her troubles were some debilitating mechanical failures. The sub might never have participated in this latest maneuver if it weren't for some daring repair work of several crewmen.

To rendezvous at the appointed time, 2200 hours on September 11, *Pampanito* sped westward at 17 knots. Four 10-cylinder Fairbanks-Morse diesel engines raised a deafening noise in the aft and forward engine rooms. When she had to dive en route, the engines were shut down and air vents closed; the smell of diesel oil mixed with the heat of the engines to produce conditions so hot and suffocating that the engineers stripped nearly to nothing.

Pampanito joined *Growler* and *Sealion* at 2130 hours and received instructions from Commander Oakley by megaphone. At 0107, radar aboard

Growler detected the Japanese convoy about 15 miles off. It was estimated that seven or eight ships were traveling in three columns with several escorts. Oakley ordered his men to battle stations: he wanted the first shot for himself. At a speed of 13 knots for *Growler* and about 10 knots for the convoy, Oakley's chance would come in less than half an hour.

Two ships in the convoy carried the POWs. Nine hundred British servicemen were crammed into the hold of the *Kachidoki Maru*, a 524-foot passenger-cargo vessel. One thousand three hundred and eighteen British and Australian men had been urged with pointed bamboo sticks to occupy the lower hold of the *Rakuyo Maru*, a similar ship of 477 feet. The two ships had left Singapore on September 6 with two tankers, two other passenger-cargo vessels and an escort of three frigates and a destroyer. They had headed on a northeasterly course for Formosa Strait; at intervals, the convoy jogged off course to confuse any tracking submarines.

Several POWs had had premonitions of disaster at sea. One of the most compelling came from Charles J. Armstrong, a 25-year-old Britisher: "I had visions of being sunk on a Jap ship and then being picked up," he recalled in *Return from the River Kwai*, a detailed account of the tragedy written by Clay Blair, Jr., and Joan Blair (1979). "I dreamed this same dream three nights before we left. I wanted to go very much and take a chance."

Shoved and prodded into the ships' holds in Singapore, the POWs concentrated on one thing only: survival. Conditions were appalling. The hatchway was cluttered with sprawled bodies; some men had passed out, others managed to groan feebly as they were trampled upon by their comrades forced to find a place among the stinking, sweating mob. Each man had barely enough room to blink. One latecomer remembers (Blair and Blair, 1979): "I fumbled and found a spot where I sat with knees drawn up under my chin and my head craned forward to avoid knocking it on the underside of the overhead."

At sea, the men were permitted to roam a designated area in the daytime under the eye of armed guards. The sunlight and fresh air helped to renew the spirit. But each night it was back into the hold, where men ill with dysentery and too weak to crawl to the toilet added to the stench.

The POWs' physical condition was far from fit even before putting to sea. In the jungles of Thailand and Burma they had lived in filthy bamboo huts, subsisted on starvation rations, suffered from malaria and dysentery and from the pain of festering sores on the skin. They had watched 12,568 fellow POWs fall dead while building the Railway of Death. Their task completed, the strongest among them were selected for transport to Japan to work in mines and factories. What followed was an interminable journey covering thousands of miles by foot, train and boat with stops at Phnom Penh and Saigon before arriving at Singapore.

Now the distance between the convoy and the first attack sub, *Growler,* was shrinking fast. Commander Oakley fixed on a tanker at the center of the column, but, when he was on the point of firing, an escort picked up on the sub, broke off and advanced menacingly. Oakley held fire and targeted instead on the approaching destroyer. At 1150 yards he let fly three torpedoes from the bow. The crew waited tensely as the seconds ticked off: 10 . . . 20 . . . 30 . . . 40. After 49 seconds the first torpedo speared the destroyer, exploded brilliantly and sent the enemy ship heeling 50 degrees to port. But the destroyer kept coming, close enough in fact to radiate heat from her burning decks to the submarine's topside. Then, at 200 yards she went under. Oakley had gambled on a risky maneuver, a bow-to-bow confrontation, and emerged the victor. As one seaman put it (Blair and Blair 1979): "It's like playing Russian roulette."

The exploding destroyer woke the POWs aboard the *Rakuyo Maru.* Their first thought: the Allies are at hand! But the excitement paled as they became aware of the destroyer glowing brightly in the darkness; the *Rakuyo Maru* might very well be next.

Oakley set his sights on two freighters, and at 0159 he released two torpedoes at each, 1900 to

Pampanito *at sea.*

2500 yards off. One freighter took two blows, the other suffered one; damage was minimal. But Commander Oakley had little time to investigate. A second Japanese escort was closing in and splashing the water with gunfire. Reacting quickly, *Growler* managed to outrace the frigate and escape to safer waters.

Sealion then took over the attack, but it was forced to retreat for mechanical repairs when its second torpedo veered badly off course. For her efforts, she was chased doggedly by a Japanese frigate.

Pampanito meanwhile had swung north of the convoy to begin her assault. After *Growler*'s attack, Commander Summers was anticipating an enemy escape to the east and moved in that direction. But the convoy shifted to the northwest, throwing off Summers' pursuit.

The next attack did not begin until 0522. Commander Reich maneuvered *Sealion* into position 2500 yards from a tanker, the second ship in the column. The torpedoes had to be set by hand because *Sealion*'s automatic targeting device had failed again. Nevertheless, all three torpedoes rocketed off and struck with precision. The tanker burned so brilliantly it threw a canopy of light onto Reich's second target: a large transport fourth in line. Three minutes after his first strike, Reich released three more torpedoes; these hurtled toward the POW-packed *Rakuyo Maru*.

Once again a fellow sub had unwittingly upset *Pampanito*'s plan of attack. Before Reich had acted, Commander Summers was preparing to fire from dead ahead of the convoy. But after Reich's first hit the convoy altered course and *Pampanito* found herself in poor position to engage the enemy.

Two of *Sealion*'s three torpedoes slammed into the *Rakuyo Maru*. The ship's bow dipped; water washed over the deck. The men clutched at railings and hatchcovers to keep from being swept overboard or slammed against a bulkhead.

There was pandemonium in the hold. But in several minutes the scrambling was over and the men tried to calculate the danger. Meanwhile, *Sealion* was being mildly reproved for her belligerence; two Japanese frigates rocked the sub with 12 depth charges. Undamaged, she descended to safe waters.

The Japanese aboard the *Rakuyo Maru* abandoned ship rapidly, taking all lifeboats for themselves; they held off the POWs with ugly bayonet thrusts and stern rifle warnings. Still, a few daring souls managed to sneak aboard. Raymond Burridge and another POW climbed up the side of a dinghy carrying two Japanese officers armed with three-foot swords. On the count of three, the two POWs flipped the boat and drowned their captors. Some men took advantage of the chaos on deck to release bottled hostility bred of two years' imprisonment and torture; they turned savage, hacking Japanese sailors to death with their own swords and strangling others.

While confusion and mayhem spread over the decks of the *Rakuyo Maru* and in the water nearby, the United States wolf pack continued to stalk the convoy, now in considerable disarray. Radar aboard *Growler* picked up signals from two escorts standing guard near the ailing ships. Commander Oakley moved to within 1650 yards and fired six torpedoes, sinking yet another Japanese frigate. With only one torpedo left in his arsenal, his patrol was over. Oakley spent the rest of the day submerged near the battle site, then was ordered to Fremantle, Australia, for refitting. Commander Reich assumed leadership of the wolf pack.

By this time, nearly all the British and Australians aboard the *Rakuyo Maru* were in the water. Staying afloat required ingenuity, strength and luck; there were no lifeboats (except those commandeered from the Japanese) and few rafts, and life jackets enough for only three-quarters of the men. Any buoyant scrap had been thrown over the side: oil drums, bamboo, timber, hatch boards. Canteens had been filled; food, cigarettes and sake appropriated. Yet once in the water some men simply panicked and went under; others could not help drifting into oil still burning on the surface. By 0600 in the morning of September 12, about 1200 surviving POWs had settled into waiting in the middle of the South China Sea. One incident related by Australian Frank Coombes in the Blairs' book (1979) set the tone for what was to come: "There was a Jap officer in the water with a couple of samurai swords hanging around his neck and about four canteens. Very friendly. He asked if he could get on the raft. One of the blokes on the raft called him over and pushed him under and held him down."

It was indeed rough going at first, especially because the Japanese had dropped some off-target depth charges in the area. The explosions jolted the floating men brutally; the force caused the walls of their stomachs to crash inward. Many men vomited, others defecated. Some did both at once while spewing blood from ears and mouth. One man was blasted out of the water, hurled several yards, then slapped back to the surface and sucked under.

None of this could be even remotely guessed at aboard *Pampanito,* where the crew was still maneuvering for its first strike. Commander Summers continued tracking the convoy through the morning hours only to surface at 1122, seemingly lost again. But by noon a spotting was reconfirmed by periscope. *Pampanito* would make its move after nightfall.

Late in the afternoon, two Japanese frigates and a merchant ship converged on the site of the *Rakuyo Maru* sinking, and rescue operations proceeded swiftly and smoothly. But there was a drawback; the POWs were excluded from taking part. Lifeboats of

Japanese survivors were emptied, and the ships sped away. One Australian recalls (Blair and Blair 1979): "We could see Japs on deck and Japs being picked up from the boats, we shouted, 'what about us?' But they just waved us away." Pick handles and baseball bats discouraged most men from clambering up the rescue ladders. A Japanese officer further inhibited the POWs by threatening to train the frigate's guns on them. A grim moment, certainly. But there was one positive note; the Japanese lifeboats had been abandoned, and they were far superior to hatch boards and oil drums. The men scrambled to climb aboard.

And so it went on into the night. Everyone wanted a spot on a lifeboat. Cries rang out from the dark sea again and again. In the end, about 30 men filled each of the 11 boats left behind. When the rearrangement had been completed, the men watched with growing despair as the Japanese rescue ships faded on the horizon. The sight broke the spirit; it was a time of many deaths. Yet from the depths of the hardy arose a strengthening of resolution. In these men was born an indomitable spirit of survival.

Pampanito, meanwhile, was playing out her own drama. By 1930 hours the sub had stalked the convoy to within 52 miles of Hainan Island. Land-based aircraft startled Commander Summers into diving twice to escape detection. Returning to the surface the second time, he had lost his prey again and it took over an hour to regain contact. Finally, at 2225, the moment was ripe for an assault. As *Pampanito* charged, a torpedo slipped its position and became trapped within its tube, threatening to explode. For several tense minutes *Pampanito's* torpedo man wrestled with the launching mechanism to stave off the sub's self-destruction. Then Summers fired on his targets: three freighters and the passenger-cargo ship *Kachidoki Maru* with 900 British POWs aboard. Nine torpedoes streamed through the water for nearly two miles. Four hit the freighters, two slammed into *Kachidoki Maru.* Fifteen minutes later the bow of the *Kachidoki Maru* pointed skyward and the ship slipped beneath the surface. About a third of the POWs never made it out of the hold. Those who did were dazed and struggled for life in the dark sea. As with the *Rakuyo Maru* disaster, lifeboats and rafts were in short supply, and the Japanese occupying most of the small craft slapped with oars at the outstretched hands of Britishers attempting to steal aboard. A thick coating of oil spread across the water's surface; oil seeped into the eyes and slid down the throat, stinging the insides. Fortunately, it had not ignited. The POWs floated on whatever wreckage was about and, to keep the spirits from plummeting, they sang such songs as "There'll Always Be an England" and "Land of Hope and Glory."

The *Rakuyo Maru* went down in the early morning hours of September 12; the *Kachidoki Maru,* near midnight of the same day. The survivors of both sinkings experienced misery that at first seemed unimaginable but by the fourth day had become commonplace. The daytime heat beat down mercilessly. Thirst was intolerable; some men made the mistake of slurping down sea water to relieve parched throats. All they gained was a moment of delirium before death. One man rose to his feet, announced he was off to milk the cows and stepped over the side. Another asked his buddies to join him at the pub and dove into the sea. A few became so violent they had to be shoved from the rafts for the safety of the sane.

Dawn of September 13 brought what survivors of *Kachidoki Maru* feared was a cruel hallucination: two Japanese frigates and a fishing trawler approaching at a distance. The ships moved in, and this time the men were liberated from the sea only to be imprisoned again by the enemy. The following day a Japanese frigate took aboard 136 survivors. A reunion at Hainan Island brought sighs of relief and frustration. On September 16, all Japanese rescue patrols were abandoned. *Rakuyo Maru* had carried 1318 POWs; the Japanese saved 136. *Kachidoki Maru* had 900 British men aboard; of these the Japanese had rounded up 520. These men were held in captivity until late August 1945. Mean-

while, somewhere in the South China Sea were 1562 men, dead or barely alive.

Pampanito continued her patrol in the hope of spotting the crippled convoy and unleashing some, if not all, of her remaining 11 torpedoes. At 1630 hours on September 14, Commander Summers made a periscope sighting of several life rafts 8000 yards off; he suspected there were men aboard but, not wanting to interrupt his tracking maneuvers, he did not investigate. After all, he assumed, they were undoubtedly Japanese. Pursuit of the convoy proved fruitless, and on September 15 *Pampanito* and *Sealion* rendezvoused; it was decided they would resume their earlier patrol of the Luzon Strait.

By this time, horrors for the POW survivors multiplied; men perished in droves. There were those whose strength finally quit, those whose courage cracked, those who were transformed into raving demons from the urine, blood and seawater they had drunk. Oil coating the eyes had plunged the lucky ones into darkness; these men were spared the sight of the blistered faces, the distended tongues and puffy lips, and the maniacal deaths.

On September 15, *Pampanito* encountered another lifeboat. The crew sped by, observed that it was unoccupied and plowed onward. Minutes later, at 1610, came the sighting that would forever color the history of *Pampanito*'s war patrol in shades of light and dark. At first, the 15 men on the rafts were

mistaken for Japanese soldiers. Summers prepared his men to eliminate the enemy. The word went out, according to one crewman, (Blair and Blair 1979) that "anyone who wanted to shoot a Jap, get a tommy gun." But as the sub swung close, the Americans could not believe their ears. Pleas of help issued from the water in English. Utterly baffled and rightfully suspicious, Summers permitted just one man to board; in the briefest of terms he learned of the tragedy at sea and immediately ordered a swift, careful rescue. Commander and crew effected this unprecedented operation with extraordinary skill. Teams were organized, swimmers risked shark-infested waters, volunteers provided emergency medical aid. The POWs' grotesque appearance and foul smell was too horrid for some *Pampanito* crewmen; most had never had to stomach the brutal side of war up close.

Summers continued to search the oily sea until dark, plucking out 9 men here, 6 men there until 73 British and Australian survivors had joined the Americans. At 1715, he radioed *Sealion* commander Eli Reich; *Sealion* rushed to the area by 1831 hours and in the hour and 25 minutes of remaining daylight saved 54 men. Nightfall forced Reich to halt rescue efforts, despite the heart-rending cries of men still in the water. But, he reasoned, he could not continue work in the dark, and if those aboard were to receive effective treatment he had to draw the line. He made arrangements for two backup subs, *Barb* and *Queenfish,* to resume the operation with expediency. Arriving in the area on September 17, the backups managed to pull 32 men to safety. *Pampanito* and *Sealion,* meanwhile, sped toward Saipan with their ailing charges.

One man aboard *Pampanito* had been schooled

in treating the sick—Pharmacist Mate First Class Maurice L. Demers, graduate of a two-month hospital corpsman school. He coordinated emergency medical procedures and aided most of the POWs himself, dispensing morphine to some and scrub downs, bouillon and toast to others. The entire *Pampanito* crew pitched in on rotating nursing shifts. Demers and staff lost only one man en route; he was buried at sea after a brief service topside.

The POWs had trouble adjusting to such concern and compassion after so long in brutal captivity. Some burst out tearfully, disbelieving it all.

Pampanito now carried 157 men in space designed for 65. Crewmen willingly gave over their quarters; some POWs were so skinny they were put two to a bunk. Several survivors were quarantined in the after torpedo room. Food and water supplies were stretched sparingly. Commander Summers made operating adjustments to compensate for the added weight, and when the sub had to dive evasively, the maneuver was executed with ease and grace and little disturbance to the patients. *Pampanito* had been on patrol 31 days; Saipan was roughly 4 days away—1300 miles.

On September 18, both *Pampanito* and *Sealion* rendezvoused with the American destroyer U.S.S. *Case* and took on medical supplies, clothing and a doctor and pharmacist. Pumped up with amphetamines, Maurice Demers had been going nonstop

for four days and three nights. But he did not feel secure in turning medical duties over to the fresh recruits. When he noticed the new doctor wasting precious time recording the POWs' names, addresses and outfits, Demers decided he'd better continue his watch. Fortunately, only six of *Pampanito*'s charges remained in critical condition.

At 0926 in the morning of September 20, *Pampanito* docked at Tanapay Harbor, Saipan. Five POWs were carried off on stretchers; the rest walked. All who made it to Saipan recovered. They were taken to the United States Army's 148th General Hospital, tears pouring from the eyes of survivors and crewmen alike. Maurice Demers missed the excitement. Still on board *Pampanito*, he had climbed into a bunk and passed out. He slept off and on for 36 hours and awoke to find he'd lost 30 pounds in five days.

Shortly, *Pampanito, Sealion, Queenfish* and *Barb*—all having discharged their POW survivors at Saipan—set off for Pearl Harbor, where the subs were checked out and the crews rewarded with two weeks' rest and relaxation at the Royal Hawaiian Hotel. Besides basking in the satisfaction of the rescue, the men could boast that their wolf packs had swept more Japanese tonnage off the water than any others to date. Summers and Reich received Navy Crosses. Demers was awarded a Navy and Marine Corps Medal and promoted to warrant

Crewmen pose aboard Pampanito's *deck.*

officer. Nearly all crewmen won some sort of decoration.

On September 28, the Australian POWs sailed directly for home aboard the liberty ship *Alcoa Polaris*. The British, dressed in United States Army uniforms, headed for Pearl Harbor on another liberty, *Cape Douglas,* on October 1. After four days as distinguished guests in Hawaii, they sailed on to San Francisco, arriving October 22. They were subjected to cramped bus tours but also managed to slip in one night of tasting the city's charms on their own. As legions of tourists and city folk know, San Francisco has always been a carouser's paradise. "You couldn't go wrong," one POW said, "what a time we had!" (Blair and Blair, 1979). It was then on to New York by train and across the Atlantic to England aboard the *Queen Mary.*

Pampanito made three more patrols before being retired to Mare Island Navy Yard at the war's end; she earned six battle stars for her service. In 1975, the United States Navy donated the historic sub to the National Maritime Museum Association, under whose direction she was refurbished and opened to the public as a museum in March 1981.

Index

Selected Bibliography

Asbury, Herbert. *The Barbary Coast.* New York: Capricorn Books, 1968.

Baker, Margaret. *The Folklore of the Sea.* North Pomfret, Vermont: David and Charles, 1979.

Blair, Clay, Jr., and Joan Blair. *Return from the River Kwai.* New York: Simon and Schuster, 1979.

Bunker, John Gorley. *Liberty Ships—The Ugly Ducklings of World War II.* Annapolis: Naval Institute Press, 1972.

Fabry, Joseph. *Swing Shift—Building the Liberty Ships.* San Francisco: Strawberry Hill Press, 1982.

Harlan, George H. *San Francisco Ferryboats.* Berkeley: Howell-North Books, 1967.

Harlan, George H., and Clement Fisher, Jr. *Of Walking Beams and Paddle Wheels.* Salinas: El Camino Press, 1951.

MacMullen, Jerry. *Paddle-Wheel Days in California.* Stanford: Stanford University Press, 1944.

McNairn, Jack, and Jerry MacMullen. *Ships of the Redwood Coast.* Stanford: Stanford University Press, 1976.

Moffat, Frances. *Dancing on the Brink of the World—The Rise and Fall of San Francisco Society.* New York: G. P. Putnam's Sons, 1977.

Newell, Gordon, and Joe Williamson. *Pacific Lumber Ships.* Seattle: Superior Publishing Company, 1960.

Newell, Gordon, and Joe Williamson. *Pacific Steamboats.* Seattle: Superior Publishing Company, 1958.

Newhall, Scott. *The Eppleton Hall.* Berkeley: Howell-North Books, 1971.

Reinhardt, Richard. *Treasure Island 1939–1940: San Francisco's Exposition Years.* Mill Valley: Squarebooks, 1978.

Riesenberg, Felix, Jr. *Golden Gate—The Story of San Francisco Harbor.* New York: Tudor Publishing Company, 1940.

Rubin, Hal. The Last of the Liberties. *Oceans,* March–April 1979, 50.

Sawyer, Leonard Arthur, and W. H. Mitchell. *The Liberty Ships.* Centreville, Maryland: Cornell Maritime Press, 1970.

Trott, Harlan. *The Schooner That Came Home— The Final Voyage of the C. A. Thayer.* Centreville, Maryland: Cornell Maritime Press, 1958.

Vickery, Howard L. Liberty Ships for Victory. Marine Engineering and Shipping Review.

Villiers, Alan. *Men, Ships and the Sea.* Washington, D.C.: National Geographic Society, 1962.

Watkins, Tom H. *Mirror of the Dream—An Illustrated History of San Francisco.* San Francisco: Scrimshaw Press, 1976.